A SECOND PONY SCRAPBOOK

Horses who write their own books

A SECOND PONY SCRAPBOOK

Another collection of bits and pieces
compiled and edited by

CHRISTINE PULLEIN-THOMPSON

Cover design by Camm Ashbrook
Associates Limited

A Piccolo Original

PAN BOOKS LTD
LONDON

First published 1973 by Pan Books Ltd,
33 Tothill Street, London SW1

ISBN 0 330 23751 9

By the same author in Piccolo
A PONY SCRAPBOOK

Made and printed by Cox & Wyman Ltd,
London, Reading and Fakenham

CONTENTS

FOREWORD

As so many of you enjoyed my first *Pony Scrapbook*, here is another book of bits and pieces. I have included some advice on building yourself a course written by famous show-jumping rider Alan Oliver; tips on jumping from Anne Bullen; quizzes from me and crosswords from Charlotte Popescu.

There's quite a lot of nonsense; as well as advice on how to treat horsy ailments from Judith Campbell; a piece on how to be a good trainer from Josephine Pullein-Thompson; the sad story of what happened to poor Jonathan and why it happened; and lots more besides.

I hope you enjoy the mixture. I hope it stops you quarrelling with your brothers and sisters (if you have any, or course!) for an hour or two, and from driving your parents mad on one of those boring days when there's absolutely nothing to do. But, most of all, I hope it makes you kinder and more understanding to that most noble animal, the British pony.

Christine Pullein-Thompson.

ACKNOWLEDGEMENTS

Putnam & Company Limited for words and drawings from *Tickner's Light Horse* by John Tickner. A. D. Peters & Company for 'There's a Pony in the Garden' from *London Pride* by Joanna Cannan, published by William Collins & Sons Ltd. Methuen & Company Limited for words and drawings from *Horse Nonsense* by W. C. Sellar and R. J. Yeatman. Blandford Press Limited for 'Jumping' from *Ponycraft* by Anne Bullen. Frederick Muller Limited for 'Fences and Courses' from *Alan Oliver's Book of Horsemanship* by Alan Oliver, and for 'An ABC of Equestrian Terms' from *Horse Sense* by Alan Deacon. The British Horse Society and The Pony Club for the illustration 'Grooming Kit' from *The Manual of Horsemanship*. Methuen & Company Limited for the use of five cartoons from *A Leg at Each Corner* by Norman Thelwell. William Heinemann Limited for 'The Wrong Bit' from *Summer at World's End* by Monica Dickens. Lutterworth Press for 'Treating your Pony's Ailments' from *Family Pony* by Judith Campbell. John Murray (Publishers) Limited for 'Hunter Trials' from *Collected Poems* by John Betjeman. The Naldrett Press for 'Pit Ponies' by F. W. Fry from *The Pony Club Annual No 3* by Alan Delgado. Josephine Pullein-Thompson for 'A Good Trainer' by Josephine Pullein-Thompson. Charlotte Popescu for three crosswords.

We regret that we have not been able to trace the copyright and source of the extract from the poem *The Hooves of Horses* by Will H. Ogilvie.

THERE'S A PONY IN THE GARDEN

from London Pride,
written just before the war, by Joanna Cannan

Lunch was early because of playing golf. It was baked eggs in dishes and then it was loin of mutton. I still like eggs in dishes because we had finished them before the awful thing happened, but never again will I really like loin of mutton. Uncle Gerald had carved and Taylor had handed the vegetables, and then she had gone out to get a clean napkin for Uncle Gerald, who said that the napkin he had been given was one of ours, just because it was slightly dirty. When Taylor came back, she gave Uncle Gerald his clean napkin and then she walked round the table to Aunt Pamela and said, 'Excuse me, madam, but there's a pony in the garden.'

It was so sudden and unexpected that my heart gave a jump and then stood absolutely still. The others told me afterwards that theirs did too.

Aunt Pamela seemed surprised. She said, 'A pony, Taylor?'

'Yes, madam,' said Taylor, 'and it seems to be doing a lot of damage. It has knocked down Master Robin's little house *and* the rose pergola.'

Aunt Pamela said, 'But I don't understand, Taylor.

Are you sure it's a pony? How could a pony have got in?'

'I'd better go and look at this,' said Uncle Gerald in manly tones, and, throwing his clean napkin on the floor though he is always telling us not to, he left the room.

Aunt Pamela looked disapproving, but she didn't say anything. I believe she thought that Taylor had gone mad and it was best not to mention it. A moment passed. It seemed like ages. Then Uncle Gerald came back again.

There's a pony in the garden

He said, 'There is a pony in the garden – a small black pony. It must have been tied to the pergola and it has pulled the pergola over and smashed up Robin's Wendy House. Where did it come from? Children, do you know anything about it?'

We swallowed our mouthfuls and said, 'Yes.'

'Well?' said Uncle Gerald in a Mr Fairchild voice.

We all said, 'She's our pony.'

'Your pony?' said Aunt Pamela. 'Where did it come from?'

John said, 'We bought her.'

'You bought her?' said Uncle Gerald. 'What do you mean by buying a pony without asking permission?'

John said he didn't know and Aunt Pamela said, 'Where did you get it?' John said, 'We bought her from a man. She was in a cart, which was much too heavy for her, and she's awfully old, so we bought her out of kindness to animals.'

Aunt Pamela said, 'Well, you've done a very naughty thing and a very silly thing too. I suppose it was the money which Lord Peveril gave you that you spent on this pony, and that was very silly because you know quite well that you can't keep a pony here. You've wasted your money and you've behaved badly, bringing a pony into the garden and spoiling everything. This isn't your house, you know. It belongs to Uncle Gerald.'

We didn't say anything. Uncle Gerald said that in his opinion we had been much worse than silly and naughty. We had been extremely impertinent and he'd like to know how we got the pony into the garden.

John said, 'Through the hall, of course. She hasn't got wings.'

Aunt Pamela told John not to be rude to his uncle, and then she said she had never heard anything like it – fancy bringing a pony into a house. Uncle Gerald said that the point was that we had no business to buy a pony without permission, much less to bring it into his house and garden. Then he said that we must have known we were doing wrong, because obviously we were trying to hide the pony.

We didn't say anything. Aunt Pamela asked Uncle Gerald exactly how much damage Pride had done and he said that she – only he very unhorsily said 'it' – had wrecked the pergola and absolutely smashed the Wendy House and trodden down everything in all the borders. Aunt Pamela said, 'Tch, tch,' and then she said that after lunch we must take 'it' straight back to 'its' master.

John said, 'How can we? We don't know his name or address or anything,' and I said, 'How could we? She's much too old and tired to work and she's half-starved and ill-treated. I thought you ought to be kind to animals.'

Then Aunt Pamela said an awful thing. She said, 'If it's in that state, the best thing would be to have it painlessly destroyed, wouldn't it, Gerald?'

We all shrieked, 'No!' but Uncle Gerald didn't take any notice. He said, 'Yes, dear; that would be best. As soon as I've finished my lunch I'll ring up the RSPCA.'

John said, 'You can't. Pride's our property,' and

Uncle Gerald asked where John had learned to be so rude, and John said, 'At school.' Uncle Gerald was furious and said that John was to leave the room without any pudding, and John said he didn't want any pudding and he left the room. I said, 'How would you like it if Aunt Pamela was painlessly destroyed?' and Aunt Pamela told me to leave the room too, so I did, and, of course, I rushed out into the garden. John was there and he had caught Pride and was petting her.

The garden *was* in rather a mess, I must say. The rotten old pergola post, which we had tied Pride to, had broken off, and I suppose she had moved away and dragged the rest of the pergola with her, and some of the wreckage had caught on the silly old Wendy House and upset it. Then Pride had evidently got her halter off – it *was* rather big for her – and, rejoicing in her freedom, she had gone for a walk round the garden, and you really can't expect a pony to know the difference between borders and paths. She had trodden on most things and the paved part of the garden was littered with the flotsam and jetsam of the pergola, so that it did look rather untidy, but, after all, it was an unforeseen accident and we should have been pleased to pay for the damage.

John said, 'Aren't they beastly?' and then he said, 'Where's the horse-rug?' I looked round and saw it. It had been trampled into a border and was rather muddy, so I shook it and then I found the surcingle and the halter and we rugged Pride up and tied her to the railings which stop you falling into the pantry area.

The next thing that happened was that Morag came

rushing out. She gave a sort of whispering shriek and said, 'He's telephoning. I thought of cutting the wires, but I don't know where they live. We *must* do something.'

Morag and I stood in the hall

John said, 'Go and hear what happens,' so Morag and I went in and stood in the hall – the telephone is in the downstairs cloakroom and Uncle Gerald hadn't shut the door, so we could hear everything. We were slightly late and he had begun, but he was still arguing. He said the pony must be taken away at once, and the RSPCA seemed to be saying that they hadn't time or something, because then Uncle Gerald asked them for the name of a reliable horse slaughterer. He repeated the unsuitable name of G. Foale and then he rang off without saying thank you, and we knew by the rustling of pages that he was looking up G. Foale's number. We heard him dial it and then there was a long silence, and then he said a word we are not allowed to say, so I suppose there was no answer owing to its being Saturday afternoon, when everybody shuts except H. Bulpit. Then we heard him dialling again and he spoke to the RSPCA and said that there was no answer from G. Foale and that he couldn't possibly wait till Monday. Of course our hearts leapt with joy – you can do a lot between Saturday and Monday – but they sank again when he said, 'Very well, but please do your utmost to come this evening.' Then he banged down the telephone thing and called upstairs to Aunt Pamela. He said, 'The RSPCA are probably sending this evening.'

Aunt Pamela came downstairs with her hat on. She said, 'Can't they come at once?' and Uncle Gerald said, 'No. As the pony isn't in pain they didn't want to come till Monday. But I was firm with them. Have you seen the garden?'

Aunt Pamela said, 'Not yet, but I'm just going to look at it,' so Morag and I rushed out and began picking up the flotsam and jetsam. Aunt Pamela stood in the doorway and said, 'Oh, dear, oh, dear,' and then she suddenly said in an angry voice, 'Where did you get that blanket?'

Morag said, 'It's a horse-rug. I took it off my bed. Of course it's rather big for Pride, but we thought we had better not cut it.'

Aunt Pamela was furious. She said it was one of her best satin-bound peach-coloured spare-room blankets and that Morag was a naughty little girl and had no business to take other people's blankets. Morag said she was sorry and offered to wash the blanket, but even that didn't pacify Aunt Pamela. She said that Morag deserved to be sent straight home to Roid and that she would write and complain to the MacAlister.

I suppose it was because Aunt Pamela mentioned Roid that I suddenly felt awful. I did wish I was there with the sea and the hills and the islands, and for grown-ups only the sensible MacAlister. I expect you will think I was silly, but I began to sniff and at the same moment Morag began to howl. Uncle Gerald said, 'Oh, for goodness' sake, let's get off, Pamela. It'll be dark before we're half-way round,' and Aunt Pamela said, 'You're all on your honour not to do anything naughty,' and they went away.

As soon as the front door had slammed, Angus appeared. He said, 'I hid, so as not to desert you in your hour of need,' and then he said, 'Dry your tears, fair maiden,' and Morag and I said we weren't fair maidens and went on sniffing and howling because it was so awful about Pride, Angus said, 'Oh, do shut up. Crying won't help. What we want is sage counsel. Has anyone got an idea?'

John said that he had been trying to think of one. We might take Pride out of London and loose her on a Surrey heath, only he thought it was about twenty miles to any suitable heath and it would take ages.

Angus said, 'Where's the New Forest?' and John said it was even farther than Surrey, and then Morag had an idea, but it was only an idea to gain time. She suggested that we should ring up the RSPCA and tell them that Mr Cadogan had changed his mind and decided not to have his pony painlessly destroyed. John said he thought it was illegal to pretend to be other people on the tele-phone, so we decided not to do it unless it was absolutely necessary to gain time. Then we all sat in gloomy silence trying to think of an idea.

I couldn't think of *anything*. I could only think of the clock ticking away the fatal moments and poor little Pride being killed instead of spending her last years in peace and plenty as I had meant her to do. She was standing patiently by the railings, and the blanket which Aunt Pamela had made such a fuss about covered her all up except for her head and her little black hoofs. I thought of all the miles she must have trotted in the service of beastly, ungrateful Man, and of course I began to sniff again, and Morag looked at me and she sniffed too. But, as the proverb says, it is always darkest before dawn, and while I had been thinking about clocks and ungrateful man and things, wiser minds had been at work, and Angus suddenly gave a shriek and said, 'I've got an idea.'

We all said, 'What?' like drowning men clutching at straws.

Angus said, 'We need a powerful ally and I've thought of one.'

We all said, 'Who?'

'He is a very powerful ally,' said Angus. 'I shouldn't think you *could* have a more powerful one, unless it was the King or Lochiel. And we have done him a service, for which he has already shown signs of being grateful. I mean Lord Peveril.'

'But he's a grown-up,' said John.

'There are *some* nice grown-ups,' said Angus.

'But wouldn't he be too high and mighty?' I said.

Morag said, 'High and mighty people are always much easier to talk to than the common herd. But of course he mayn't be horsy.'

'All the nobility and gentry are horsy,' said Angus.

'But what could he do?' asked John.

'Don't you see,' said Angus, 'he probably has vast estates and acres and acres of lush meadows, shaded by immemorial elms and bordered by rippling streams. He could send Pride down to his vast estates and keep her there until Tony marries an MFH and has an estate of her own.'

'He could, but I don't suppose he would,' said John.

'Well, I propose that we go and see him,' said Angus. 'I'll do the talking, if you'll come.'

John said, 'I'm not coming. I think it's a silly idea.'

'Very well,' said Angus. 'I'll go alone. And John Carey, who, except for Morag, is my nearest kinsman, can stay in the nursery like a baby with Robin and read in the newspapers the fate of his Chief.' This – as I expect you know – sort of comes out of the historic scene between Prince Charlie and Lochiel, and I said, 'Though not another man in London shall draw a sword, I will come with you.' And Morag said that if we looked in vain for her, we were to search where the dead lay thickest, and then John said he supposed he might as well come too. I said I had better wash, as I had got rather dirty picking up flotsam and jetsam, but Angus said we mustn't waste time in case Lord Peveril was going to the House of Lords. We took a short farewell of Pride and then we rushed out into the Square.

A moment later we were standing on Lord Peveril's doorstep and ringing his bell. The door was opened by the stately butler. When he saw us he smiled benevolently, and Angus, in a polite voice, said, 'Is his lordship at home?'

The butler said that his lordship was having lunch, and Angus said, 'We don't want to disturb him, but will you say that we have come on a matter of life and death, please.'

The butler said he would inquire and would we come in? He ushered us into a large hall, where there were chairs and things, and we sat down. Angus, who was being very grown-up, said, 'That's a nice Raeburn over the mantlepiece.' Of course, he only knew it was a Raeburn because there was a brass label on it which said so.

The butler was away for ages and John said perhaps we had better go. Morag scornfully asked what he was afraid of, and John said he wasn't afraid of anything but he was sure that Lord Peveril would think we were silly. Just as he said that, Lord Peveril appeared. He was tall and stately, and wore an eyeglass and black clothes.

We all leapt to our feet and said, 'How do you do?' Morag said she hoped that Lord Peveril had had a nice lunch, and Lord Peveril said yes, thank you; he had had grilled sole and some Cheshire cheese. Morag said that cheese made her dream, and Lord Peveril said lobster was the only thing that made him dream. Morag said that she hadn't had lobster since she came to London, but she often had it at Roid and, of course, it was lovely there, because it came straight out of the sea. She asked if Lord Peveril liked champagne and he said he preferred a good burgundy, and then he asked her if she liked tapioca pudding, and really, we thought they would never stop talking about food, and they didn't until Angus interrupted Morag, who was telling Lord Peveril how to make scones. Angus said, 'I hope you don't mind us calling without an appointment, but we are in sore need of a powerful ally, so we thought of you.'

Lord Peveril said that he was flattered and what could he do for us? Our hearts leapt with joy as he said that he was very grateful to us about the burglar and would do anything in his power.

Angus said, 'I'm afraid it's rather a long story. Shall I begin at the beginning and go on to the end?' And Lord Peveril said, 'Yes, do.' So Angus began with my buying Pride and he told Lord Peveril how we had kept her in the Square garden and all the details, even about the blanket off the spare-room bed. When he had finished the story he went straight on and said, 'Our idea was that, if you would be our powerful ally, you could save

the life of a noble animal and put us for ever in your debt
by sending Pride down to your vast estates and letting
her live there till Tony marries an MFH.'

Angus stopped. For an awful moment Lord Peveril
didn't say anything. Then, to our joy, he said that he
could see no possible objection to our excellently
thought-out plan.

We all said, 'Hooray,' and Lord Peveril said that he
had better telephone to his stud groom and have a horse-
box sent up at once from his Berkshire place. It wasn't a
very vast estate, he said, but there was a park of forty
acres where Pride could live with a very old and nice
Dartmoor pony, which had belonged to his son. He rang
the bell and the butler came, and Lord Peveril told him
to telephone and tell the stud groom, and then to telephone to the RSPCA and tell them that they weren't
wanted at Mr Cadogan's house after all. Then he said he
thought he had better write a note to Aunt Pamela and
explain. We agreed that it would be a good thing, so he
wrote the note and we all said, 'Thanks *awfully*,' several
times. We asked if he would be there when the horse-box
came, but he said unfortunately not; he had got to go to
a silly conference about dull things. Then he said that
next week he would be down at his Berkshire place and
we must all come and spend the day and see Pride. We
accepted with pleasure and then we tactfully got up to
go.

Lord Peveril came to the door with us. As we crossed
the hall Angus said, 'That's a fine Raeburn, sir,' and
Morag said, 'This is quite a nice house for a London
one.' Though our cousins live miles from anywhere and

A nice Dartmoor pony . . .

never see any one, they are much better at polite con-
versation than we are.

Well, we rushed home, and of course we rushed
straight to the garden and broke the good news to Pride.
As there was now no need for concealment, we went
down to the kitchen and persuaded Cook to let us make a
bran mash. While the kettle was boiling we rushed
across to the Square garden and got the bran, oats, chaff
and hay: we thought we might as well save our bene-
factor some money by sending the remains of everything in the horse-box with Pride. As we came back we
saw Lord Peveril getting into a stately black car, which
John said was a Rolls-Royce. Of course we waved madly
to him and he waved too.

When we got back the kettle was boiling, so we made the bran mash and left it with the folded kitchen table-cloth over the top of the bucket to steam. Then we thought we had better make Pride look tidy for the stud groom, so we groomed her, and Angus and Morag pulled her mane, and John and I got some salad oil and oiled her hoofs. Then Nanny tapped at the window, so we fetched the bran mash and then we went in to tea.

At tea Nanny and Robin were awful. Nanny gave us a lecture on worrying our poor Aunt Pamela, and Robin said, 'Fancy spending your money on a nasty dirty pony! I've got ten shillings in my money-box and five pounds three shillings and ninepence in the Post Office, haven't I, Nanny?' And Nanny said, 'Yes, darling – you're Nanny's sensible boy.' We told Robin he was a beastly stingy pig and a miser like Uncle Ebeneezer in *Kidnapped*, but he didn't take any notice, so I threw a macaroon at him. It didn't hit him, but he began to cry and Nanny said she would tell Aunt Pamela. As soon as she said that, Robin stopped crying and began to grumble about his Wendy House, and Nanny said, 'Never mind, darling. The nasty little pony is going to be shot this evening.' She looked awfully surprised when we all started giggling, and after a bit she went and looked out of the night-nursery window – I suppose our giggling made her wonder if we had taken Pride away and hidden her. Though our legs were weak from giggling, we seized the opportunity to get down and rush back to the garden.

Lord Peveril had told us that it would take about two hours for the horse-box to come from his Berkshire place, so, allowing a few minutes for the stud groom to wash and brush his hair and put on his coat, we expected the horse-box about five. It was five now, so we thought that, as stud grooms are always busy, what with strangles and staggers and fistulus withers, not to mention glanders and grease and seedy toes and cracked heels and poll evil, we had better have Pride ready and waiting in the Square. She had finished her bran mash, so we put on her halter and led her through the hall – she

We expected the horse-box about five

looked sweet blinking in the sudden blaze of light after the darkness of the garden. She didn't like going down the steps much, but we coaxed her with horsy voices and a macaroon.

After that there was nothing to do but to wait for the horse-box. We walked Pride up and down in case of pneumonia, and after ages and several false alarms, we saw, by the fitful light of the street lamps, a large and looming vehicle turn into the Square. We all shrieked 'Horse-box!' and this time it really was the horse-box. It stopped in front of Lord Peveril's house, and we ran and Pride trotted up the Square.

When we got to Lord Peveril's house the stately butler

We ran and Pride trotted up the Square

had come out and was standing on the pavement talking to the stud groom, and another man was opening the horse-box and letting down the ramp. The stud groom was awfully agreeable. He said this was the pony, was it, and he remarked that we had wrapped her up well. We said he must excuse her rather unhorsy horse-rug, as it was really only a blanket off the spare-room bed, and he laughed and said that he betted that had caused it, by which he meant that he betted it had caused a row. Morag said that if you had a blanket it was a much better deed to use it for a cold little pony than for a fat person, who came to stay and had a hot-water bottle as well, and the stud groom said that she was quite right and then he said that he had brought a pony rug, so we took off the blanket and put on the pony rug, which was lovely; it was a dark-blue day rug with yellow binding and the initials of Lord Peveril's son and heir. We scarcely recognized Pride in it – she looked so fashionable – and the stud groom said that when she'd fattened up a bit she'd look OK and she'd be a nice companion for Daydream. Of course we asked about Daydream and he told us that she was a dark bay Dartmoor pony with a mealy nose; in her young days she could jump as high as her ears and used to buck off Lord Peveril's son. I said I hoped she wouldn't despise Pride, and the stud groom said he expected she would be only too glad to have another old lady to gossip with about the good old days. Then he said he must be getting on, so I said I would lead Pride into the horse-box. She went in like a lamb, and the stud groom tied her up in a professional way so that she shouldn't shake about. We took a short farewell of her and then, while the other man was closing up the horse-box, we shook hands with the stud groom and said good night and thanks awfully and that we hoped we should see him again soon. A moment later the horse-box started up and Pride was on her way to the forty-acre park where she would wander at will in knee-deep grass for the rest of her days.

QUIZ 1   WHICH ONE IS RIGHT

1. Is a hackamore:
   - (a) A kind of hack?
   - (b) A moorland pony?
   - (c) A bitless bridle?

2. Is a stifle:
   - (a) A hood used to quieten a restless horse?
   - (b) A joint on the hind leg?
   - (c) A kind of twitch?

3. Is a drench:
   - (a) Something you give to a horse with colic?
   - (b) A kind of bit?
   - (c) A grooming tool?

4. Who said, 'No foot no 'oss.'
   - (a) John Jorrocks in a book by Surtees?
   - (b) John Manly when Black Beauty broke his knees?
   - (c) Harvey Smith when Mattie Brown hit a fence at Wembley?

5. Is Monday Morning Disease caused by:
   - (a) Too much galloping?
   - (b) Too many late nights?
   - (c) Too rich food and too little exercise?

6. Is laminitis:
   - (a) A special liniment for cracked heels?
   - (b) A kind of numnah?
   - (c) An inflammation in the hoof?

7. Is a calkin:
   - (a) A heel on a horse shoe?
   - (b) Another name for a rubber bit?
   - (c) A brand of horse nuts?

8. Is a habit:
   - (a) Another name for a surcingle?
   - (b) Clothes worn when riding side saddle?
   - (c) A muzzle used to cure crib biters?

9. Is a liver chestnut:
   - (a) A chestnut horse with a bad liver?
   - (b) A bad liver caused by eating a chestnut?
   - (c) A dark chestnut horse?

10. Is a rowel:
   - (a) Part of a spur?
   - (b) Slang for rowdy horse?
   - (c) A martingale with three rings on it?

11. Is navicular:
   - (a) A special girth for fat ponies?
   - (b) A special winch for picking up dead or ill horses?
   - (c) An incurable disease of the hoof?

12. Does 'on the bit' mean:
    (a) That a horse is very fit?
    (b) That a horse is going well with plenty of impulsion?
    (c) That a horse is getting old?

13. Is a 'half pass':
    (a) To move a horse diagonally sideways?
    (b) A wink from one horse to another?
    (c) A horse half way through his prime?

14. Does 'to peck' mean:
    (a) A horse that pecks at his food?
    (b) A horse which makes faces at other horses?
    (c) A stumble, usually after a jump?

15. Is a coffin bone:
    (a) A bone in the hoof?
    (b) A horse's hoof used as a paper weight?
    (c) The shortest rib?

16. Is a dam:
    (a) A natural water jump?
    (b) A wisp used wet?
    (c) A mare used for breeding?

17. Is the near-side:
    (a) The side of a horse nearest you?
    (b) The left side of a horse?
    (c) The side of a loose box nearest the door?

For the answers please turn to page 136.

HORSES TO AVOID

Here, from Horse Nonsense *by Sellar and Yeatman, are some faults to avoid at all costs when buying a pony!*

The full set of (four) feet

There is an old saying, 'No foot, no horse'; so you will naturally refuse to buy any horse which has not the full set of (four) feet.

You will also avoid 'U-Necked' or 'V-Necked' Horses (very discouraging) and those dangerous 'wall-eyed' animals (which go about looking for walls to dash into or smash your legs against), and, above all, the rare but permanently discouraging stamp of horse known as a 'Strawberry Roach'.

You will remember also that a good horse, though it

need not be a thorough-bred, must be 'sound' in the legs,
or steady on its thorough-pins as horsemen say, and also
'sound in wind', by which horsemen mean that its

breathing should make no noticeable sound at all, as a
horse which 'whistles' is rather irritating, particularly if,
as so often is the case, it *always whistles the same tune*.

Then, of course, there are the questions of *Age* and
Lameness. Everyone knows what a bore it is trying to
help lame dogs over stiles; heaving lame horses over five-
barred gates is, as any hunting-man will agree, a *posi-
tively crashing bore*.

You should therefore avoid purchasing any horses
which are warranted to be permanently lame, in spite of
what Capt Pontoon* (*Dirigible Quadrupeds*, p 109) says

*Capt W. D. Pontoon, MC, BSA, RE, author of *Dirigible Quadrupeds*, etc.

about horses which are permanently lame on three legs being curable by deliberately laming the fourth leg, '*thus rendering them, in effect, sound*'. Cap P., as everyone knows, is himself by no means a sound authority.

Finally, the question of Age. Everyone knows that the way to tell if a horse is too young or too old is to look at its teeth, and that the older the horse the longer the teeth and, of course, vice versa.

Too young   *Too old*

CROSSWORD 1

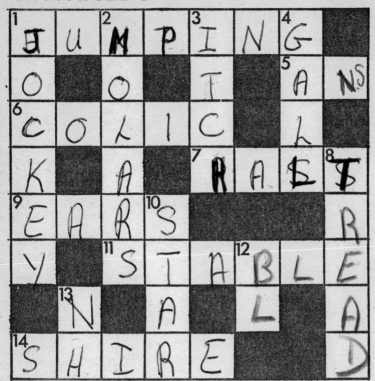

ACROSS

1. Slowly — has become a great sport (7)
5. '— hounds ran' means the distance they covered (2)
6. Pain in the belly (5)
7. half — (4)
9. We have them too (4)
11. A building for housing horses (6)
14. A breed of heavy horse (5)

DOWN

1. Rider of a racehorse (6)
2. The large grinding teeth of which there are 24 (6)
3. Swat — (4)
4. Sore place under the saddle or girth (4)
8. Self-inflicted wound on the coronet (5)
10. White mark on the forehead (4)
12. Abbreviation for black (2)
13. Initials for National Hunt (2)

Answers on page 142.

T—B

THE GOURMET

There once was a pony called Polly,
Who ate nothing but peppermint lolly,
She turned a strange green,
Was a sight to be seen,
And was sent to a zoo for her folly.

(Moral: Don't feed your pony on what you like yourself!)

JUMPING

Some useful advice from the famous pony expert and pony illustrator Anne Bullen

Miss D. Mason on Tremella

Jumping very low obstacles should be part of the early training of both horse and rider.

The rider's body should be supple and with his pony; the hands should be carried low on either side of the pony's neck. Use the legs to get the pony well up to the bit at the trot or canter. As the pony takes off over the fence, allow him to stretch his head and neck by giving your hands, but maintaining contact with the reins; bring your hands back to the normal position as he lands.

You must learn to tell your pony when and where to take off at each fence. There is a principle of counting three – two, one OVER – for three strides when you present your pony at the fence. This you can only learn by constant practice. An extra squeeze is necessary as the take-off signal to your pony. Watch experts jumping and see if you can spot this timing and extra squeeze.

There are numerous ways of schooling jumpers – many excellent and some cruel, but the guiding principle for the ordinary rider is straight-forward and clear.

Jumping low fences on the lunge

Start with a pole on the ground, lunge your pony over this till he is calm and unfussed, then raise the pole and do the same. Lunge him over all sorts of different-looking obstacles – the more Heath Robinson-looking the better – but always very low. For a young pony, a foot or eighteen inches is not too low to start with. Lunge him with the rein fixed to the cavasson ring, or on a halter or head collar – never on the bit. Experts can do so if they wish, but this book is not a guide for experts. A jerk in the mouth when jumping will soon put your pony off. Even if it does not stop him jumping, it will make him

Full of confidence

throw up his head. This hollows his back, which lowers his hind quarters, and so spoils the pony's style of jumping, which will make him hit the fence behind.

To jump correctly, the pony must lower his head and

neck and get his weight forward. He should look at his take-off – hence the importance of a good ground line, and jump with a rounded back.

He should describe an arc over the obstacle. This is the correct style for show jumping and cross-country

Major L. Rook on Starlight

jumping, and you must have this picture in your mind when schooling your pony on the lunge. The jumping in the Grand National is something quite different, magnificent though it is; but you must remember that they can brush through six inches to one foot of the National fences, and you have to teach your pony to clear each fence.

When your pony is going well, out hacking, and obeying the aids reasonably well in the school, start riding him over his jumps.

Remember he has got to adjust his balance to carry your weight over the jumps – up to now he has jumped free. Therefore make it easy for him. Start at the beginning over poles on the ground and gradually raise them. Start by riding at all your low jumps out of a trot. Circle round and round, in and out of your jumps – then pop over one, circle again, pop over another two, and so on, always calmly, and reward him when he does well. Let the whole lesson be enjoyable for both of you.

Be sure to have your neck strap in your hand for the

Cross country

first few lessons. Some youngsters jump very awkwardly, and if you get out of time and left behind over the jump, your hands may fly up, and you risk giving your pony a jab in the mouth.

Wide fences and spreads are better for your pony than lots of upright ones, as they make him extend himself;

you can see from the sketches that he will have to jump higher in order to clear the greater widths. This is the best method of schooling your pony to jump heights.

Some wide fences have to be jumped out of a canter. When your pony jumps a varied and low course out of a trot, jump some of the fences out of a canter, then more trotting. He must learn to be completely obedient and jump at whatever pace you wish.

If you start by trotting over low fences, halting and standing still, and then going on over the next fence, you prevent your pony getting hotted up and disobedient. On the other hand, if you start by cantering on at one fence after another before your pony is completely obedient, well-schooled, and handy, he will soon get hotted up and over-keen and start rushing his fences. He is then getting rapidly spoilt.

After you have had a little experience, you will realize that to canter fast round a really twisty course and meet each fence correctly, and to time your jump right, is a very difficult art and wants a high degree of training and practice.

By all means take your pony out hunting – it will be good for both of you. Never school all the time – hack or hunt in between. Galloping on at natural fences will be a good experience for both of you. The good groundwork you have given your pony at home will help him to be clever and handy, and you will both have the greatest fun in the world.

Just one word of warning about jumping while out hunting. Don't ride a blown pony at fixed timber. Let him get his wind first, otherwise you risk a nasty fall.

Wire is another menace, and you must see that the fence is clear if you get there first, maddening though it may be. Horses can jump wire, and do so; but first they have to be safe clean jumpers, and you must have experience and know what you are doing before you take on wire fences and wire oxers.

When your pony has hunted and has had some experience, take him to shows, hunter trials and rallies. Have as much fun as you like and get all the practice you can,

Never be tempted to take on four- or five-foot jumps too soon

but be careful when jumping not to over-face your pony. Ponies can jump incredible heights and enormous fences, but first let them be experienced and full of confidence. This comes in the second year of your training, and you can then launch out and jump in every competition you can get into.

Remember, however good and promising your pony, start the right way and stick to your principles of training. Don't be led astray by people laughing at you, because you will only start him jumping by taking him over small obstacles.

Never be tempted to take on four-foot or five-foot jumps too soon. Your pony may even jump them once or twice, and then he will begin refusing. Once that happens you have started spoiling him.

FENCES AND COURSES

Some more advice, this time from Alan Oliver, the great show-jumping rider

Forget the show-ring type of fences, painted in beautiful red and white stripes; forget the cleverly designed walls which look as though they have been imported direct from the Yorkshire Moors. Their only purpose is to brighten up the scene at public events – and to give the televiewers added variety as the camera swings over the ten or twelve jumps in the ring.

All you really need is an object that will encourage your horse or pony to leave the ground for a short while. And the materials for such a construction may be found in profusion in the countryside.

Let's assume that you have a paddock or small space at your disposal, somewhere away from traffic and not too frequently used by hikers, cattle, or small children. Look around you, at the spinney over there, at the hedges, at that old barn – branches of dead trees, brushwood, logs, twigs of all sizes and varieties lie about just waiting to be used for building small jumps.

Now, before you start piling up your building materials in a haphazard barrier, let us inquire further into the few, but very necessary, rules of building up an obstacle. We've agreed that the primary object of a fence is to encourage the horse to move skywards whilst in motion. But as with the first manned rocket to outer space, the burning problem is that of a safe return to earth.

This safe return can be jeopardized in several ways. An open invitation to disaster is of course, to build too high in the initial stages of training. This often causes a mount to refuse, a habit that is extremely difficult to cure. Jumping beyond the ability of horse and rider will inevitably result in a loss of style and confidence, to say nothing of injuries.

If your obstacle is placed too near a hedge, for instance, allowing an insufficient getaway run, the horse may be wary of taking it and check or run out. After all, he will be able to see beyond the jump and may object to running full tilt towards a thorny hedge!

Uneven ground may throw the horse off balance. Rabbit holes or clefts in the soil can be dangerous, so check the area before you before deciding on the location of the jump.

Make your construction simple. This is not a battle-course in which you wish to test the nerve of yourself and your mount, so let there be no unpleasant surprises for him as he jumps. Walk the horse up to the obstacle before you attempt to take him over, and let him have a look at it. You'll find that he'll be much more confident once he has inspected the hazard.

Now to building your first jump: many of the materials, as I have said, are easy to find, and to these you may add your own special building material, namely straw bales. Place two bales about ten feet apart on their sides, and lay a rough pole or branch across the top. Here you have a near-perfect eighteen-inch jump. For added solidity put down a ground-line. This consists simply of another pole placed on the ground at the base of the obstacle, at the forward edge. A novice mount invariably jumps a fence from a position which is too close for normal show jumping purposes. The ground line fools him into jumping a little earlier. Look at the jumps when you next go to a show – you'll see that most of them have well-defined ground lines, put there to help the horses.

Stage two in your progressive exercises can take the form of a spread jump. Move the single pole to the edge of the straw bales and place another one at the other edge. Now you have a spread of about two feet six inches. Work at this jump until both you and the horse are confident that it presents no difficulties.

Later turn the bales up on end and construct a higher jump on them, using an extra set of bales if you think you are ready for a spread at that height.

In constructing these improvised fences, remember that the wider you can make the obstacle, the less likely is your horse to 'run out' or swerve to the side. And the higher the jump the wider it should be, because although the horse may apply himself to the smaller barriers with apparent willingness, he may check or object in some other violent way to a jump which requires more energy to surmount.

As a further preventive to possible running out, heavier and larger wings can be attached to the fence. Two or three bales piled up on top of each other make a simple and effective way of doing this. Or oil drums can be placed at the limits. If you find that your horse regularly knocks down the bar of the jump, the fault may lie in its flimsy construction. The horse, a wily animal, knows very well that it is easier to jump *through* a thin fence, so add a few hedge trimmings, or twigs to the base-line to give the obstacle a greater appearance of solidity.

As your skill increases, something a little more 'professional' will be required. The simple hurdle is the answer. Cheap, lightweight, easy to transport, it is a most useful piece of equipment in the training of horse and rider. Solid in appearance, a hurdle is nevertheless easily broken – an important point when hit by a flying rider. Most hurdles have sharp stakes at the base which can be easily jabbed into the ground. An inaccurate jump merely knocks the hurdles out of their position.

LAYING OUT A PRIVATE COURSE

Your course plan should be simple. The complicated weaving and double-tracking seen at the shows are usually the result of restricted space or the desire of the course builder to use several fences more than once.

Your own course could be set out in a simple figure-of-eight. Alternating the hurdles with your 'natural' fences, the upright jumps with the spreads, a very useful and instructive course can be laid out with a maximum of about eight to ten jumps. A combination fence (i.e. two fences close together) could be incorporated as your expertise increases.

Remember to allow plenty of turning-space when you

change the direction of the route; your mount will be moving at a speed that will necessitate a turning circle of about fifty feet. Anything sharper than that will cause a decrease in speed and an awkward approach-line to the next jump.

In the initial stages, at least, the distance between the jumps should be as great as the available space allows. Combinations should be spaced accurately to suit the stride of the horse. They must be placed to permit the horse to take a single complete stride – or two strides – between them. A suitable distance between two four-foot fences of a combination is twenty-one feet for a pony, and twenty-four feet for a horse. If the distance allows only a part-stride to be taken, the second fence will inevitably spend most of its time on the ground.

After several hundreds of hours of diligent practice (and make no mistake, it will take a considerable time) on your private course, when the secrets of balance, rhythm, and muscular co-ordination have been learned, then *and only then* may you consider making your first public appearance in the show ring.

TEST YOUR KNOWLEDGE

Here are a set of grooming tools. Do you know their names, the use of each one and why you groom your pony?

Answers on page 140.

BASIC EQUIPMENT

Some basic items which you will need to buy or borrow before or when you acquire your first pony

Somewhere to keep him, (a garden isn't big enough!), with a good supply of clean, clear water (a bucket isn't big enough!)

Halter or headcollar

Bucket

Feed-bin

Haynet

A supply of hay (if winter)

Pony nuts and/or oats

Salt lick or rock salt

Straw, shavings, peat moss or sawdust if stabled, plus fork, broom, shovel and wheel-barrow for mucking out

Well-fitting saddle and bridle

Set of grooming tools (see previous page)

A basic first-aid kit is also useful. Here are a few suggestions.

Cotton wool

Lint

Bandages, including stable and crepe

Kaolin paste or animal lintex

Antiseptic

Eye ointment
A pair of blunt-ended scissors
Some mackintosh or plastic
Fly deterrent
A puffer of antiseptic dusting powder
A veterinary clinical thermometer

Don't try to use the thermometer alone, and remember, better than all home remedies is a vet, so *do* call one for all but the most minor injuries and ailments. Never forget the saying, 'A little learning is a dangerous thing'.

And now some more items, though not quite so basic, which you must acquire soon after the arrival of your pony.

The address of a good blacksmith and vet
Tack cleaning materials
Saddle soap
Metal polish
Sponges, dusters and cloths
Hoof oil and brush to put it on with
Saddle horse or bracket
Hook for bridle
Somewhere to keep your equipment (the kitchen isn't always popular!)

And later, when you become smarter:
Tail and leg bandages
Rugs of all kinds
Tail guard and knee caps for travelling
Here's some advice from famous cartoonist Norman Thelwell on the difficult art of grooming

Use the body brush vigorously – he will enjoy it

Polish his coat with a rubber

CROSSWORD 2

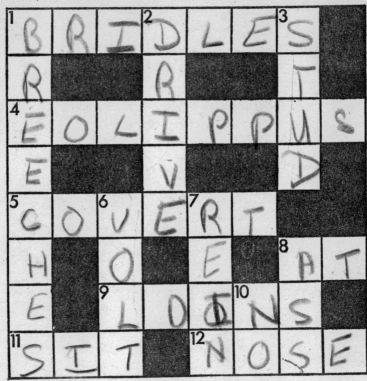

B	R	I	D	L	E	S	
R			R			T	
E	O	L	I	P	P	U	S
E			V			D	
C	O	V	E	R	T		
H		O		E		A	T
E		L	O	I	N	S	
S	I	T		N	O	S	E

ACROSS

1. Saddles and — (7)
4. The first equine ancestor (8)
5. A wood where hounds may look for a fox (6)
8. 'Over — the knee' (2)
9. Part lying behind the saddle (5)
11. How you — is important in dressage (3)
12. It may be a Roman one (4)

Answers on page 142.

DOWN

1. Worn with hunting boots (8)
2. You could be in a cart or a car when you — (5)
3. Mares, foals and Stallions are kept here (4)
6. The name of a small circle in equitation (4)
7. Part of the bridle (4)
8. She or Jack — (3)
10. Is dishing a vice (2)

AN OLD WAR HORSE

In this extract from Black Beauty *by Anna Sewell, Captain describes the life of a war horse nearly a hundred years ago*

Captain had been broken in and trained for an army horse; his first owner was an officer of cavalry going out to the Crimean War. He said he quite enjoyed the training with all the other horses, trotting together, turning together, to the right hand or to the left, halting at the word of command, or dashing forward at full speed at the sound of the trumpet or signal of the officer. He was when young a dark, dappled iron grey, and considered very handsome. His master, a young high-spirited gentleman, was very fond of him, and treated him from the first with the greatest care and kindness. He told me he thought the life of an army horse was very pleasant, but when it came to being sent abroad, over the sea in a great ship he almost changed his mind.

'That part of it,' said he, 'was dreadful! Of course we could not walk off the land into the ship. So they were obliged to put strong straps under our bodies, and then we were lifted off our legs in spite of our struggles, and were swung through the air over the water, to the deck of the great vessel. There we were placed in small, close stalls, and never for a long time saw the sky or were able to stretch our legs. The ship sometimes rolled about in high winds, and we were knocked about and felt bad enough. However, at last it came to an end, and we were hauled up and swung over again to the land. We were very glad and snorted and neighed for joy when we once more felt firm ground under our feet.

'We soon found that the country we had come to was very different from our own, and we had many hardships to endure besides the fighting. But many of the men were so fond of their horses that they did everything they could to make them comfortable, in spite of snow, wet, and all things out of order.'

'But what about the fighting?' said I. 'Was not that worse than anything else?'

'Well,' said he, 'I hardly know. We always liked to hear the trumpet sound and to be called out, and were impatient to start off, though sometimes we had to stand for hours waiting for the word of command. When the word was given, we used to spring forward as gaily and eagerly as if there were no cannon balls, bayonets, or bullets. I believe so long as we felt our rider firm in the saddle and his hand steady on the bridle, not one of us gave way to fear, not even when the terrible bombshells whirled through the air and burst into a thousand pieces.

'I and my noble master went into many actions together without a wound. Though I saw horses shot down with bullets, pierced through with lances, and gashed with fearful sabre cuts – though we left them dead on the field, or dying in the agony of their wounds, I don't think I feared for myself. My master's cheery voice as he encouraged his men made me feel as if he and I could not be killed. I had such perfect trust in him that while he was guiding me, I was ready to charge up to the very cannon's mouth. I saw many brave men cut down, many fall mortally wounded from their saddles. I had heard the cries and groans of the dying, I had cantered over ground slippery with blood, and frequently had to turn aside to avoid trampling on a wounded man or horse, but, until one dreadful day, I had never felt terror. That day I shall never forget.'

Here old Captain paused for a while and drew a long breath. I waited, and he went on.

'It was one autumn morning, and as usual an hour before daybreak our cavalry had turned out, ready caparisoned for the day's work, whether it might be fighting or waiting. The men stood by their horses waiting, ready for orders. As the light increased, there seemed to be some excitement among the officers, and before the day was well begun, we heard the firing of the enemy's guns.

'Then one of the officers rode up and gave the word for the men to mount, and in a second every man was in his saddle, and every horse stood expecting the touch of the rein or the pressure of his rider's heels, all animated, all eager. But still we had been trained so well, that, except by the champing of our bits, and the restive tossing of our heads from time to time, it could not be said that we stirred.

'My dear master and I were at the head of the line, and as all sat motionless and watchful, he took a little stray lock of my mane which had turned over on the wrong side, laid it over on the right, and smoothed it down with his hand. Then patting my neck, he said, "We shall have a day of it today, Bayard, my beauty, but we'll do our duty as we have done." He stroked my neck that morning more, I think than he had ever done before, quietly on and on, as if he were thinking of something else. I loved to feel his hand on my neck, and arched my crest proudly and happily; but I stood very still, for I knew all his moods, and when he liked me to be quiet, and when gay.

'I cannot tell all that happened on that day, but I will tell of the last charge that we made together. It was across a valley right in front of the enemy's cannon. By this time we were well used to the roar of heavy guns, the rattle of musket fire, and the flying of shot near us; but never had I been under such a fire as we rode through on that day. From the right, from the left, and from the front, shot and shell poured in upon us. Many a brave man went down, many a horse fell, flinging his rider to the earth. Many a horse without a rider ran wildly out of the ranks, then terrified at being alone with no hand to guide him, came pressing in amongst his old companions to gallop with them to the charge.

'Fearful as it was, no one stopped, no one turned back. Every moment the ranks were thinned, but as our com-

rades fell, we closed in to keep them together. Instead of being shaken or staggered in our pace, our gallop became faster and faster as we neared the cannon, all clouded in white smoke while the red fire flashed through it.

'My master, my dear master, was cheering on his comrades with his right arm raised on high, when one of the balls whizzing close to my head struck him. I felt him stagger with the shock, though he uttered no cry. I tried to check my speed, but the sword dropped from his right hand, the rein fell loose from the left, and sinking backward from the saddle he fell to the earth. The other riders swept past us, and by the force of their charge I was driven from the spot where he fell.

'I wanted to keep my place by his side and not leave him under that rush of horses' feet, but it was in vain. And now without a master or a friend, I was alone on that great slaughter ground. Then fear took hold on me, and I trembled as I had never trembled before. I, too, as I had seen other horses do, tried to join in the ranks and gallop with them, but I was beaten off by the swords of the soldiers. Just then a soldier whose horse had been killed under him, caught at my bridle and mounted me, and with this new master I was again going forward. But our gallant company was cruelly overpowered, and those who remained alive after the fierce fight for the guns, came galloping back over the same ground.

'Some of the horses had been so badly wounded that they could scarcely move from the loss of blood; other noble creatures were trying on three legs to drag themselves along; and others were struggling to rise on their forefeet, when their hind legs had been shattered by shot. Their groans were piteous to hear, and the beseeching look in their eyes as those who escaped passed by and left them to their fate, I shall never forget. After the battle the wounded men were brought in, and the dead were buried.'

'And what about the wounded horses?' I said. 'Were they left to die?'

'No, the army farriers went over the field with their pistols, and shot all that were ruined. Some that had only slight wounds were brought back and attended to, but the greater part of the noble willing creatures that went out that morning never came back!

'I never saw my dear master again. I believe he fell dead from the saddle. I never loved any other master so well. I went into many other engagements, but was only once wounded and then not seriously. When the war was over, I came back to England, as sound and strong as when I went out.'

I said, 'I have heard people talk about war as if it was a very fine thing.'

'Ah!' said he. 'I should think they never saw it. No doubt it is very fine when there is no enemy, when it is just exercise and parade, and sham fight. Yes, it is very fine then; but when thousands of good brave men and horses are killed or crippled for life, it has a very different look.'

'Do you know what they fought about?' said I.

'No,' he said. 'That is more than a horse can understand. But the enemy must have been awfully wicked people, if it was right to go all that way over the sea on purpose to kill them.'

DO'S AND DON'TS WHEN SELLING YOUR PONY

Sadly, sooner or later most of us have to sell a pony. Below are a few tips

Don't sell your pony in a hurry.

Don't tell lies about him.

Don't sell him to someone who can't control him.

Don't send him to a horse sale unless he is completely unreliable.

Don't sell him to someone too poor to pay for his hay in winter (i.e. a friend who plans to feed him out of his or her pocket money).

Don't sell an old pony to a riding school where the work is hard, or to someone keen to ride every day and all day.

Don't sell a young unschooled pony to an inexperienced rider unless there is an experienced person to help.

Don't sell your pony to someone too large or too heavy for him.

Don't sell your pony to anyone likely to sell him for meat.

Don't ever forget what you owe to the pony who taught you to ride.

Do groom your pony and see that his shoes are on and in good order before the arrival of a prospective buyer.

Do clean your tack and be well-turned-out yourself.

Do be honest; it will pay in the long run.

Do ensure that a well-bred pony will have a stable or shelter in winter.

Do make certain he won't be over-fed (i.e. that he won't be given the freedom of fifty acres of lush grass if liable – and most small ponies are – to develop laminitis or sweet itch as a result).

Do try and visit your pony after he has been sold.

Do find out everything you can about his new owners before you part with him.

Do put a happy and suitable home before all else – even money!

HOW TO GET RID OF YOUR HORSE

More useful advice on how to sell your pony, by John Tickner

Perhaps the most difficult thing connected with horses is getting rid of them. Now that you know all about horses and your own has several times got rid of you, you will undoubtedly want to get rid of it. The most sensible way of getting rid of your horse is selling it at a profit. It is certainly not much use trying to give it away, particularly in your own county, because you will find that everyone knows all about it and won't even look it in the mouth.

You may at first think that the best thing to do is to get into touch with the hairy old dealer who sold you the animal. This, however, will prove pointless because the dealer will either have shaved by now and consequently be unrecognizable, or will find a lot of things about the horse that have deteriorated since you have had it, such as its wind, its manners, its vices and even its pedigree.

The wisest plan is to advertise in special horse newspapers which are read only by horses and hounds and horse people and hound people. Before you do this you must be familiar with some of the correct horse selling terms and what they mean. The following are some useful definitions:

IDEAL FOR A BEGINNER: The horse doesn't know anything either, so they might as well learn together.

Easy to catch

SUITS ELDERLY GENTLEMAN: At his age nobody much minds what happens to him anyway.

HAS BEEN REGULARLY HUNTED: Particularly by the owner who has had to chase it all over the county.

QUIET WITH HOUNDS: A valuable animal because it can take a sly kick at them without neighing with laughter and attracting the attention of the Master.

EASY TO CATCH: Stands over the rider whenever it has bucked him off.

SOUND: Sings, whistles and roars.

WILL JUMP ANYTHING: Especially out of its field, its rider, horse-show judges and spectators.

LIVES OUT: Spends most of its time in other people's fields and gardens.

Lives out

LIVES IN: Confirmed cadger; difficult to keep it out of the kitchen.

GOOD DOER: Will do anybody it can lay its teeth on.

Almost any horse can be placed in one of these categories and all you have to do, once the advertisement has been paid for, is to retire, like a spider into your web, and wait for your first victim. In due course one will arrive and ask to see the creature. The horse, not expecting visitors, will be looking its worst, not even having done its hair.

The victim begins to examine it, going first to the front end to look it in the eye. This he finds difficult

Good doer

because the eye keeps rolling. Behind the victim's back you try frantically to put the horse in a pleasant mood by indicating that you have some sugar. The animal, which appears even dumber than usual this morning, suddenly gets the idea, takes a step forward on to the victim's toe and butts him over with its great ugly head.

Removing the horse's other hoof from the victim's face you extract him from beneath the animal and remark that it is amazingly gentle with children.

Now comes the awkward moment when the victim will drift around to the rear end, unaware of the awful danger to which he is exposing himself. You try hard to keep him otherwise occupied but he insists on a close inspection of the hind legs.

You retrieve the victim from the spot, fifty yards away, to which he has suddenly and unwillingly gone, dust him down and ask him if he would like to ride the beast. Although by now he is looking doubtful and beginning to mutter that he is not sure that it is quite what he wanted, he plucks up courage and says, yes, he would like to get on its back.

A saddle is fetched, up gets the prospective purchaser and so does the horse. You remark that he is a bit keen, hasn't been out much recently, too much corn, etc. Horse and rider go round the field and when the horse comes back you light a cigarette and wait for the rider. The thing to do now is to imply that he voluntarily dismounted, and you must do this quickly, before he has time to make any comments himself. You will probably have the initiative anyway, because his mouth will most likely to be full of turf.

When he can speak again, he will do one of two things. He will either go off in his car without speaking at all, or buy the brute for a quarter of the price you paid for it.

Some people advocate leaving the stable door or paddock gate open as a means of getting rid of a horse and shutting them smartly when the animal has gone.

This only works when you don't want to get rid of your horse. It is surprising how a really large horse that gets out against your wishes can walk along main roads, through towns and farmyards, remaining invisible, whereas a horse you desperately want to lose is spotted at once by the local constabulary or even by small children, and brought back before it has had time to go a few hundred yards. Even worse, some horses hang around just outside the door or gate, refusing to go away at all, and so you have to let them in again.

Lending a horse you don't want doesn't work either. You will soon find that people will not return books or lawn mowers but never forget to return a horse, particularly at the end of the summer. This is probably because books and lawn mowers don't eat. No, it is absolutely useless going all Shakespearean and shouting 'Farewell the neighing steed!' because it is ten-to-one the brute will soon be neighing away again on your premises, the middle of the night being a favourite time.

When one really considers the whole subject of human relationship with horses one becomes aware that, after all, the initiative is mostly with the horse and that it is the horse who gets rid of the rider when he decides to do so.

QUIZ 2 YOU NAME IT

1. The smallest breed of pony.
2. The comb used for cleaning a body brush.
3. The horny growth on a pony's leg.
4. The bone above the fetlock.
5. Chopped up hay and/or straw.
6. A female pony.
7. Another name for a hunting tie.
8. A back that is concave or dips.
9. The outer part of the hoof.
10. Hocks which turn inwards.
11. Shoeing with cold ready-made shoes.
12. A narrow chested horse without much bone or substance.
13. An instrument used for measuring horses.
14. The part of a pony in front of his rider.
15. The moss used for bedding.
16. The natural food of a horse.
17. A horse which can gallop long distances without tiring.
18. A tool used for picking out hoofs.
19. A horse of 14.2 or under.
20. A sore made by the rubbing of a girth.
21. The place where followers, hounds and huntsmen collect before a hunt.
22. An artificial aid attached to a rider's boot.

23. The place at which a horse is measured.
24. A soft swelling around the fetlock often caused by work on hard ground.

Answers on page 136.

THE WRONG BIT

Read what happens when Cassie puts a pelham on her pony's bridle in this extract from Summer At World's End* *by Monica Dickens*

Carrie got on Peter in the yard and walked round, not touching his mouth. He fussed with the bit and shook his head, clinking the curb chain. When she pulled him in gently, he resisted. She pulled a little harder. When he felt the pinch of the chain under his chin, he threw up his head and backed wildly, through the manure heap, knocking over a wheelbarrow, scattering chickens and pigeons, and missing by inches the sun-bathing tortoise.

Yesterday he would not back at all. Now he wouldn't stop. He finally backed himself into the wall, crashing a pile of flowerpots, and Carrie got quickly off. What now?

Lester turned up at World's End most afternoons, dropping casually out of a tree, or coming through a hedge from the wrong direction, or hopping down from the back of a passing lorry. He had said, 'If you're going to put a curb on him, you're not going to ride him.' So when Carrie heard the scolding of blue jays from the corner of the beech wood, which meant that Lester was

*Also available in Piccolo Books.

coming through that way, she led Peter out of the gate and into the field across the lane, mounted, used her legs as hard as she dared, and rode off out of sight round the hill.

She rode Peter with a very light contact, hardly feeling his mouth. He flexed, stepped out, trotted beautifully, with his head steady and his fine ears forward. She was right! She rode in joy, singing.

They hopped through the gap in the hedge at the top of the hill, and on to the huge flat expanse of grass that had once been a Fighter airfield, long ago in the War. Peter took hold. She pulled him in. As soon as he felt the curb, he started to back again. He backed into the hedge and stopped, trampling, nervous and excited, between desire to gallop, and fear of the bit.

'Come on, Peter!' Carrie used her legs and slackened the reins. With a jet-propelled thrust of his quarters, he was off with her, over the broken macadam of the old runway, past the tumbledown Air Force sheds, across another runway, galloping much too fast over the long uneven grass.

Carrie had once ridden a racehorse, and found out there was no way to stop. If you pulled, the racehorse went faster, leaning against your hands. The same thing was happening with Peter. The more she pulled, the more he pulled against the hated bit, fighting away from the pain, setting his jaw and his neck so that she couldn't even turn him in a circle.

At the top of the airfield, there was a narrow track under trees to the common. Carrie leaned forward under the clutching branches. Peter went faster. He burst out on to the common, swerving round gorse bushes, jumping them, floundering through a boggy place and out on to firm ground on the broad track that led to the road. Carrie pulled. She prayed. She begged Peter. To her shame, she realized afterwards, she had shouted and wept.

Being run away with is a black madness of despair. The horse is your fate, and your fate is out of control. Galloping crazily, Peter dashed her under a tree at the edge of the common, slid down a bank, landed on the road to the roar of a motor-cycle and stumbled and fell as the motor-cycle swerved, just missing, and roared on.

Peter scrambled up at once. A few yards away, Carrie got up slowly, shaken and battered, and shook her fist after the dwindling motor-cyclist. It wasn't his fault. But he might have stopped. But she was glad he hadn't. One side of her face was scorched and grazed. The eye was closing. Dirt was in her mouth. Her teeth felt loose, and her brain felt looser. Her legs felt as if she had been in bed for a week.

She would have to lead Peter home. She limped over to him and reached for the reins. He flung up his head and cantered off down the road, stirrups bumping and flying.

She walked for a long time. When anyone came by, she turned away her face and stood still, so that they would not see her limp. She felt that she must look as dreadful as she felt. They would rush her off to the hospital. Doctors would prod her bones. They would pull down the blinds and say she had concussion. It would all be more than she could bear.

Trudging along with her head down and aching, her knee hurting so badly that she began to be sure that she would never run, or even walk again, she thought dark and bitter thoughts, while low clouds swirled up the valley and began to spread downwards in fine misty rain. She would be a cripple for life. She would be in a wheel chair, her shoulders powerful as a man from turning the wheels. She would be like that lady who went on riding after a crippling fall in a point-to-point. They would have to dig a pit for John to walk into, so that she could slide on to his back from her wheel chair. Would she get a medal? What for? She had been a fool, not a heroine.

She heard the sound of hoofs without looking up. Who cared? Other people went riding. Other people had horses. Quiet, well-mannered horses who couldn't canter a hundred yards without blowing and slowing, let alone gallop against a curb for miles and miles.

The hoof beats came nearer, came round a corner. Carrie turned and began to walk in the other direction, so that they would not see her grazed and swollen face.

'Carrie!'

She turned. It was Michael on Oliver. Lester was with him, riding Peter bareback, in a rope halter.

'You're going the wrong way,' Michael said with interest. 'Were you knocked silly?'

Carrie hung her damp hair, but Lester got off and came to her, leading Peter, and put her hair gently back behind her ears to see her face.

'You really did it this time.' His dark eyes searched the damage.

'What does it look like?'

'As bad as it feels.'

Michael was chattering away, asking a hundred questions, whistling at her smashed face, predicting that she had broken her knee, lost the sight of her eye, would catch murder from Tom, would have to wear a veil for the rest of her life, like that old lady at the Golden Age Home who had fallen into the fire . . .

Lester did not say anything. He gave Carrie a leg up on to Peter's short strong back, and hopped up in front of her. Clinging round his thin waist, she was too weak and dizzy to ask him if he thought it was safe to ride double on Peter.

Michael jogged beside them on Oliver's short spry legs, trotting when they walked fast, rising very high and quick in the saddle like an animated toy, asking questions which Carrie only half heard, drowsily, with her head lolling to the rhythm of Peter's long walk.

When they were almost home, she heard a voice which must be her own, thick out of a swollen mouth.

'If Peter goes so well for you in a halter,' she said to the back of Lester's dark alert head, 'it won't matter only having one bridle. We can ride together now.'

POOR JONATHAN!

A short cautionary tale with a very sad ending, by Christine Pullein-Thompson

'Hurry! It's a marvellous day for a ride,' cried Jonathan, leaping out of bed.

His mother had breakfast waiting for him in the kitchen.

'What do you want in your sandwiches?' she asked when he appeared, dressed in riding clothes.

'Ham. I told you so yesterday. Don't you ever listen?' said Jonathan rudely.

He ate cornflakes, bacon and eggs and toast and marmalade. Ten minutes later he was outside feeding hay and whole oats to his elderly grey pony Seagull.

'We are going to be out all day – and we're going to meet Peter and Charles on Frencham Common,' he told Seagull. 'We shall go on the greatest ride there ever was.'

Seagull gobbled her unaccustomed bucketful of oats while Jonathan groomed her. He picked out her hoofs and oiled them before going indoors to change into riding boots. His father had already left for work. His mother handed him a packet of sandwiches. 'I'll expect you about four then,' she said.

'Yes, or later still. It depends on how far we go and whether we get lost,' replied Jonathan.

'Well, don't stay out after dark, please, Jonathan,' pleaded his mother.

Seagull was still eating hay when Jonathan tacked her up. His mother waved when he left. It was a perfect day for riding. The sky was full of small moving clouds; a light breeze fanned Jonathan's face. What a day for January, he thought pushing Seagull into a trot.

'Come on, let's go!' shouted Peter

It was six miles to Frencham Common. Jonathan had only allowed an hour to get there. Seagull was drenched with sweat when he arrived and his friends were waiting for him.

'At last!' cried Peter. 'Come on, let's go!'

'Race you across the common,' shouted Charles.

They galloped away through the bracken, jumped gorse bushes, forced their ponies through ditches. Their ponies were bigger and younger than Seagull. Jonathan could feel his pony tiring, but he didn't want to spoil the fun, so he pushed her on with his legs.

'Get on! Keep going you old nag,' he shouted pretending to be a cowboy. 'Bang! bang!' he yelled. 'Hi, you guys wait for me!'

They left the common and rode across plough land into woods where trees had been felled and the mud was knee high. They galloped across empty fields where the wind cut through them and dried the ponies' sweat.

Jonathan never knew how far they rode altogether; but it was almost dark when he parted from his friends on Frencham Common. Mum will be furious, he thought, forcing Seagull into a trot. It will be pitch dark in a minute.

The weather had changed. There was ice on the puddles now and a clear night sky. Slowly the moon rose.

Jonathan's mother was waiting for him outside the house in the road.

'Are you all right?' she called.

'Yes, only stiff and cold and my hands are freezing,' shouted Jonathan.

'Hurry in and get warm then. I'll run a bath and put some mustard in it,' said his mother turning towards the house.

Jonathan turned Seagull into the paddock. She was still sweating. He fetched her hay and another bucket of whole oats. He patted her.

'Take it easy now,' he said. 'You can have a day off tomorrow. You can have the whole day to yourself, you deserve it.'

He ran indoors to his hot bath to be followed by an

enormous high tea. Sometime later when he was comfortably installed in front of the television set, his father came in.

'So there you are,' he said. 'I've just been to see Seagull. What water she had was frozen over. She drank three bucketsful straight off, poor little thing. When did you last water her?'

'She had some this morning. I'm sure of that,' said Jonathan, not moving his eyes from the screen. 'Look at this programme Dad. This is how it's going to be in twenty years' time . . .'

'She drank like a fish,' his father said.

Next morning everything was white with frost. Jonathan woke late. He was pleasantly tired and his bed was warm and comfortable. It was a long time before he got up.

His mother called. 'I haven't fed Seagull, Jonathan. Daddy said you were to do it. It's nearly ten o'clock. Come along, dear, get up.'

'All right, I'm getting up, don't nag,' shouted Jonathan.

'She was waiting at the gate two hours ago.'

'I'm coming!'

He spent a long time dressing. 'I must have something to eat first,' he said appearing in the kitchen at last. 'What is there? I'm jolly hungry.'

He ate a good breakfast. His comic had arrived so he read that too before he went outside to feed Seagull.

She was not waiting at the gate any more and she didn't whinny when she saw him. She was walking up and down the paddock with a wild look in her eyes. She kept stopping to roll over and over in the white frosted grass like an animal gone mad.

Jonathan shouted, 'Seagull! I'm here! Seagull, breakfast!' But she didn't raise her head to look at him. 'Seagull, what's the matter?' he shouted and all the time he could feel his heart sinking further and further into his wellington boots, until at last he turned towards the house crying, 'Mummy, Mummy. Seagull's gone mad. She doesn't know me. She's got rabies or something.' And now he was crying on and on as though he would never stop.

'She was all right at eight o'clock.' His mother was in a pinny and bedroom slippers.

'Do something. Get a vet,' yelled Jonathan. 'Please.'

He went back to the field. He stood and prayed that Seagull would get well again. He remembered yesterday and how hard he had ridden. He wanted to say 'I'm sorry.' But she wouldn't look at him.

His mother came back. 'There's one coming at once,' she said. 'He said we were to keep her walking up and down.'

Jonathan fetched a halter. But Seagull would not stand still and he could see nothing but agony in her eyes and his own were blinded with tears.

'I can't get it on,' he said. 'Can't you see, Mummy! Do something please . . .'

His mother held out a carrot, but Seagull was not interested in carrots any more. 'I wish the vet would come. Why doesn't he hurry?' asked Jonathan. 'She's going to die. I know she is.'

Seagull sank to the ground. Her whole body was soaked in sweat. Her legs quivered as she tried to roll once more. Then she lay her small elderly head on the frosty ground with a sigh and simply stopped breathing.

'She's dead,' Jonathan said.

A minute later the vet arrived. Jonathan was crying too much to speak.

'You're too late, she's dead,' said his mother and he saw that she was crying too.

The vet climbed the paddock fence. He looked at Seagull. Jonathan looked away. 'I should say she twisted a gut,' he said after a time. 'She must have had a very bad attack of colic, poor little thing. When did you first notice she was ill?'

He looked at her water which was frozen solid; his eyes scanned the paddock for a sign of hay.

'She was all right yesterday,' said Jonathan's mother. 'Jonathan rode her all day.'

'She's quite old, of course, and old ponies do get chills easily, which can lead to colic,' said the vet climbing back over the fence. 'You don't want a post-mortem do you? I'll send the knackers round; they won't be long.'

In the distance a clock struck one. Jonathan thought his life would never be the same again. His pony was dead. What had he done wrong?

See if you can think where Jonathan went wrong, then look at page 138 to see if you're right.

TREATING YOUR PONY'S AILMENTS

Some useful advice on an important subject by Judith Campbell

BROKEN KNEES

If your pony falls on the road he may damage his knees. This can mean anything from scraping off the hair without breaking the skin to a deep wound. If the skin is not broken or only lightly scratched, the knees should be bathed with warm water and a little, mild antiseptic. This should be done by squeezing cotton-wool or a cloth above the knees, so that the water trickles down over the wounds. With this type of damage a few days' treatment of bathing, together with some soothing ointment to keep off the flies, should be all that is necessary, and the hair will grow again.

With deep or extensive cuts, send for your vet. He will prescribe treatment, and give the pony an anti-tetanus injection unless your pony has already been immunized – always a very wise precaution. If the knees are badly cut there may be a permanent, hairless scar, but with rest and correct treatment there are unlikely to be any other ill effects.

COLIC

Colic is a pain in the tummy.

It can be caused by a variety of things, such as unsuitable food, a chill, or even grazing sandy soil so close that a quantity of sand enters the stomach.

It can be mild and intermittent when at intervals the pony appears ill at ease, looks at his flanks, and may kick

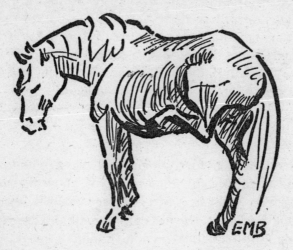

The pony may kick at his tummy if he has colic

at his tummy. If it is acute he will probably become frighteningly violent, throw himself to the ground as the spasm catches him and literally drip with sweat. Whatever form the colic takes, send for your vet at once.

The old method of treatment used to be a 'colic drink', but nowadays the vet gives an injection which acts much more quickly and is easier to administer.

My husband's enthusiasm for giving colic drinks was

damped some years ago when Blaze, as usual, was the patient. The pony was highly strung and never very easy to cope with, and I was trying to insert the neck of the bottle into his mouth behind the incisors, whilst my husband held his head up at the correct angle. Unfortunately something went wrong with the operation and the entire drink, of a delectably sticky green, cascaded down inside my husband's coat sleeve.

While you are awaiting the vet it is a good idea to walk the pony quietly around on grass until his arrival. This may prove impossible in cases of acute colic but, although it is all right for the pony to lie down, he should not be allowed to roll in case he twists a gut.

COUGHS

The first treatment for a coughing pony is to send for the vet and refrain from riding until you know the cause. With a very mild case of coughing which is likely to continue for weeks, the vet may sometimes allow quiet hacking. But if a badly coughing animal is given fast or strenuous work, he may end up with broken wind and become virtually useless.

There are many different causes of coughing, perhaps the most common being an infection that sometimes appears to be air-borne. Animals who have had no contact with other horses or ponies may suddenly contract it. A pony who lives out is likely to throw off his cough more easily than if he were stabled.

The vet may give you a liquid cough cure for your pony or what is called an electuary. Both will have directions on the bottle, and the liquid is usually given twice daily, mixed in the feed. I hesitate to tell you the following story as it is very much against myself, but it does illustrate the fact that one should use one's common sense.

When we first had Twala he was coughing, and the vet sent along a liquid cough mixture, with 'One Teaspoonful to be given Twice a Day' written on the bottle, but no further directions. Why it didn't occur to me to put it in his feed I don't know. Maybe because it was summer time and he was not officially receiving any dry food, but twice a day I solemnly opened Twala's mouth and poured in a teaspoonful of cough mixture! Perhaps it explains some of our ridiculous regard for him when I add that, equally solemnly and with evident relief, he swallowed it – and his cough got better.

An electuary is a paste, based on black treacle. It can be smeared on the pony's tongue with the aid of a smooth piece of wood or the back of a small wooden spoon, or you can use your fingers. Gently pull out the tongue through the side of his mouth and, once the paste is on, open his mouth wide as he draws in his tongue again – otherwise he may scrape it off with his lips and teeth.

CRACKED HEELS

This condition occurs on the heels and back of the pastern, and often on the coronet as well. The pony may go very lame, and the sores may turn a bluish-green tinge. First signs of cracked heels can usually be cleared up by applying daily a little soothing, preferably antiseptic, ointment – Dettol is as good as any – but different ponies react to different remedies. If the sores do not quickly heal, or if they show signs of spreading, the vet should be called in at once as complications can be dangerous.

Cracked heels are caused by softening of the skin from persistently wet and muddy conditions, or from frost, so it occurs chiefly in the winter. Leave your pony's heels untrimmed through the wet and cold weather; the hair is nature's protection against diseases such as this.

GIRTH GALLS

These can be caused by a too tight or too loose girth, or by a stiff leather girth that has not been kept supple. They are more likely to occur when the pony is in soft, grass-fat condition. Prevention is much better than cure, and the use of a properly adjusted nylon girth is likely to keep you out of trouble.

Watch for the first signs of a girth gall and then treat it as you would any small wound. A strip of cotton-wool or lint wound round the girth should prevent it making things worse, but if the gall is large or raw the pony must not be ridden until it has healed.

LAMENESS

A pony can go lame from a variety of causes, but nine times out of ten the seat of the trouble is in the foot. To begin with you have got to decide on which side he is lame. If you realize that he will 'drop' on to the sound leg because he doesn't want to put weight on the one that hurts, you can see which it is as he is trotted towards you. Lameness behind is not so easy to spot but, watched from the back as the pony trots away from you, the same rule applies. If you still can't make up your mind, ask your helper to turn him quickly after trotting away from you, and you should see the pony 'drop' on to his good leg.

Perhaps you are out riding and your pony suddenly goes dead lame. In this case he has probably picked up a stone in his foot. Jump off quickly and have a look. Sometimes an awkwardly shaped stone becomes firmly wedged between the shoe and the frog, but with the aid of a stout piece of stick you should be able to dislodge it. Quiet walking for a little while after the stone is out is usually all that is necessary, but if the sole of the foot has been bruised your pony may be tender on it for a day or two.

The trouble is likely to be much more serious if he picks up a nail. If you are a long way from home you should seek permission to put him in a nearby field until some form of transport can be arranged. Send for the vet immediately, and he is pretty sure to want the black-smith to come along and remove the shoe. If not immun-ized, the pony should have an anti-tetanus injection, and the vet will probably tell you to poultice the foot.

This treatment can be carried out even if you have nowhere to shut the pony in. Warm some Kaolin paste, spread it on a piece of lint or clean cloth and place over the wound. Then wrap the whole foot in another large piece of cloth. A layer of cotton wool comes next, then

A poultice for a pony that has picked up a nail

more cloth big enough to reach well over the fetlock. Tie all this, firmly but not too tightly, with tape round the pastern; and make sure the knot rests on the side of the leg. Then get hold of a sack cut it down a little and draw it over the hoof so that the foot, dressings and all, rest in one corner. Pull it up and wrap round the leg and secure again with tape, below the knee and round the pastern. Once more these fastenings must be firm without being tight, and knots and fastenings must never rest on tendons or ligaments. The top of the sack should be turned over like a stocking, and the whole effect is that of a clumsy boot. The pony will infuriate you by clumping round his field and wearing out the sack, so be prepared to use up several, and renew the dressing once a day, until there is no heat in the foot.

If your pony goes lame almost immediately after

being shod, a nail may have been driven too close to the sensitive part of the foot. Have the shoe removed, and the treatment is the same as for picking up a nail. If he has been shod after losing a shoe some days before and comes out of the blacksmith moving rather as you might in a pair of tight new shoes, he may only be footsore. In this case there should be little or no heat in the foot, and the symptoms will gradually fade out. But if they persist for more than twenty-four hours you should consult your blacksmith. He will not remove the shoe in a case of footsoreness, as this would only aggravate the trouble.

Your pony, and particularly if he's a young one, may throw a splint. This is a small, bony lump which may form on the splint or cannon bone. These lumps are painful while forming and can cause lameness, but seldom give trouble once they are there. The vet may prescribe a 'working' blister. This is usually a liquid which is brushed or rubbed on the affected part. It causes no pain, will not remove the hair and the pony can still be worked while it is being used – but not, of course, if he is already lame. Frequent hose-piping, in which a stream of cold water is directed on to the injured part of the leg, is alway good treatment in cases of lameness and especially where there is any strain, swelling, or heat.

Your pony may be frightened of the hosepipe to start with but, if you reassure him by voice and begin by playing the water gently on to his hoof before either moving up the leg, or increasing the pressure of water, he will soon get used to it. Twenty minutes twice a day is not too long to spend in hose-piping.

LAMINITIS

You should suspect this form of foot fever if you find your pony standing on his heels, with his hind feet under his body to take the weight. He will be in obvious pain and reluctant to move. The condition is most likely to appear with the coming of the lush spring grass, and small fat ponies who receive insufficient exercise are most prone to it.

There is an old saying to the effect that if you can get your pony to the end of June without developing foot fever, he's safe for the rest of the year. Like most sayings there's a grain of truth in it, but you should watch his bulk all through the summer. It is asking for trouble to graze ponies on clover leys.

If your pony does show signs of laminitis, send for the vet, have his shoes removed, and greatly restrict his grazing. Cold water – hose-piping or standing him in it – will help the pain in his feet.

Many people naturally dread parting with an old or out-grown pony and prefer to pension him off. But personal knowledge of two beloved ponies who both, through lack of work, developed laminitis so badly that they had to be put down prompts me to suggest that a new, kind home is far better treatment.

RUNNING NOSE AND/OR EYES

Grass-fed ponies are not prone to colds, but they do occasionally catch them from other ponies. Unless the weather is exceptionally cold and wet, your pony is likely to throw off this type of infection more quickly if he is not brought inside. He should be watched carefully and, if he appears obviously unwell or has a thick discharge from the nose, your vet should be summoned. Normally the infection will run its course, but nasal discharge can be a symptom of more serious trouble.

A running eye is sometimes caused by a blocked tearduct, and your vet should be able to deal with this.

TAIL AND MANE RUBBING

There is an unpleasant skin disease called sweet itch, which is caused by an allergy. In this the pony rubs portions of himself quite raw during the spring and summer months, and I hope you will never have to deal with it. Many grass-fed ponies do rub off the hair on the tops of their tails, and sometimes their manes as well, and this gives them a very scruffy appearance just when you want them to look their best for the Easter and summer holidays.

Occasionally rubbing of the tail is due to irritation caused by worms, or by minute mites on or under the skin, but often it is caused, as with sweet itch, by an allergy – although in a milder form.

It is not an easy condition to cure, especially as different ponies may respond to different remedies. Your vet will be able to light on the right one for your pony. A mixture of powdered sulphur and oil is often effective, and is certainly so in Twala's case. The vet will provide this if he thinks it likely to be of use, and the mixture should be shaken vigorously before applying.

Wash the mane and tail quite free of scurf. Occasionally, where the scurf is bad, this can contribute to, if not cause, the rubbing. In this case a daily egg-cupful of linseed oil, given in any sort of feed, will help to clear up the scurfy condition – and make your pony's coat shine. Green soap or a pure toilet variety make good shampoos. Rinse thoroughly, and when the hair is dry rub some of the oil and sulphur mixture well into the roots of the hair. This remedy should be applied once or twice a week, and it may be necessary to continue the treatment all through the summer months. It is a messy process, but at intervals and before any special occasion the mane and tail can be washed clean of the preparation.

TEETH

Sometimes a pony seems to have difficulty in chewing, drops food from his mouth, or mysteriously goes off his food. In this case you should ask your vet to examine his teeth. They may be jagged or uneven and be causing him pain.

If the pony is quiet, the vet will probably ask someone to hold the tongue out of the way while he rasps the teeth even with a big file. If your pony won't allow this or any other necessary medical treatment, he may have to be twitched.

A twitch consists of a loop of thick string attached to a stout, short stick. The string is placed high over the pony's top lip, and the stick twisted until the pressure is just sufficient to take the pony's mind off anything else.

Personally I have always found that given a quiet vet with a way with his animal patients, family ponies have such faith in the human race that they make no fuss at all, and a twitch is totally unnecessary. But if a pony is restive it must be restrained for its own safety.

WORMS

However well you feed and look after your pony you may find, particularly in the winter, that he still looks 'poor' and thin, and has a staring, lacklustre coat. The cause can easily be worms.

Ponies normally have a certain number of these parasites but it is when there are too many that trouble arises. Various kinds of worms infect horses, but red worm usually produces the most ill effects, especially in young animals. The worms are invisible to the naked eye and your vet may ask for a sample of fresh dung. Alternatively he may suggest giving a powder that deals with all types of worm present.

The dose can consist of one powder, or of several to be given on consecutive days. It may have to be given in a mash, or mixed into a feed of oats and bran. And this is one occasion when cubes are no use, except to sprinkle on top as an appetizer.

Some ponies seem undiscriminating and will happily gollop up anything, worm powder included, but others are suspicious by nature and refuse to touch the feed. If you suspect that your pony is going to be difficult, shut him in or tie him up for some hours without food beforehand. With a really awkward customer let him go

hungry all day. Then make up a large and really tempt-
ing feed, add shredded carrot and a little sugar or salt,
mix in the worm powder thoroughly and all should be
well.

It is a good practice to dose your pony for worms in
spring and autumn, as a matter of routine. But choose
suitable weather when it is not too wet or cold.

And now from Thelwell a little more about pony ailments!

If he is constantly trying to scratch himself, suspect skin trouble

And if he rolls about, it is probably colic

HUNTER TRIALS

by John Betjeman

It's awf'lly bad luck on Diana,
 Her ponies have swallowed their bits;
She fished down their throats with a spanner
 And frightened them all into fits.

So now she's attempting to borrow.
 Do lend her some bits, Mummy *do*;
I'll lend her my own for tomorrow,
 But today I'll be wanting them too.

Just look at Prunella on Guzzle,
 The wizardest pony on earth;
Why doesn't she slacken his muzzle
 And tighten the breech in his girth?

I say, Mummy, there's Mrs Geyser
 And doesn't she look pretty sick?
I bet it's because Mona Lisa
 Was hit on the hock with a brick.

Miss Blewitt says Monica threw it,
 But Monica says it was Joan,
And Joan's very thick with Miss Blewitt,
 So Monica's sulking alone.

And Margaret failed in her paces,
    Her withers got tied in a noose,
So her coronets caught in the traces
    And now all her fetlocks are loose.

Oh, it's me now. I'm terribly nervous.
    I wonder if Smudges will shy.
She's practically certain to swerve as
    Her pelham is over one eye.

      *   *   *

Oh wasn't it naughty of Smudges?
    Oh, Mummy, I'm sick with disgust,
She threw me in front of the Judges,
    And my silly old collarbone's bust.

PIT PONIES

An ever-dwindling number of ponies still work in our pits. F. W. Fry tells you how they lived and worked in 1952

Some people cannot believe that a pony, worked underground and deprived of light, can be happy and contented. They believe that ponies become blind after living in the mine for some time, but this is not true. Working and living in artificial light does not appear to affect the eyesight, and when ponies are brought to the surface their eyes seem to be quite normal. It is, in fact, illegal to work a blind pony underground.

No pony is allowed to work in a mine under the age of four, and it is not usual to employ mares underground. About half the ponies are geldings and the remainder stallions – and lively little chaps they are, too. They are bred mostly in North Wales or the Shetland Isles, but for some reason Dartmoor and Exmoor ponies do not make good 'pitmen'. Before the war some came from Russia and Iceland.

On arriving at a colliery, the young pony is trained firstly by lunging in a strong halter or musrole. He is mouthed by being tied with pillar reins in a stall for a short time each day; then he becomes accustomed to wearing harness and finally he is yoked with the harness and taught to pull a small truck or 'tub' as it is called. All this usually takes about six or seven weeks, and then the pony is sent underground. There is always plenty of room in the pit cage which conveys miners and equipment underground, and at some collieries there is a special box fitted inside the cage which takes the pony.

The pony is taken to work by an experienced trainer chosen for his patience and skill. The trainer will take the new arrival to a quiet part of the mine and gradually and gently accustom him to the conditions. This second period of training varies according to temperament but on an average it continues for two months. As soon as the pony has proved to be satisfactory, he is clipped all over – including his mane and tail – the latter being clipped quite close, which would look very funny to you but makes for coolness and cleanliness.

The pony is seldom out of his stable more than about six-and-a-half hours a day for five days in the week, with an occasional shift on a Saturday morning. The tub which the pony pulls generally holds about half a ton of coal and runs on iron rails. The driver, who is known as a 'putter' usually squats on the limbers, which are light detachable shafts secured to the pony by harness. The putter has to crouch down so as to avoid catching his head or back on the roof. No harm will come to the pony, because he's not allowed to go into places where the roof is too low. The pony pulls the tub – empty – into the coal face, a distance of from 80 to 150 yards, although this distance varies depending on circumstances. On the return journey he pulls out a tub which has been filled by a coal hewer or filler. About thirty-five such

Pony correctly yoked; shoulder chains in line with the limbers, and bearing chains not too tight

journeys make a day's work and if you are clever at problems that concern ponies pulling tubs x yards in y hours, you will have calculated by now that the pony does – roughly speaking – a six-mile journey each day. As the tub is on rails it runs smoothly and is probably nothing like such hard work as that experienced by a costermonger's pony who works in the open air.

When the putter or driver eats his sandwiches half-way through the 'shift' the pony has some chopped hay and water. The pony makes it quite clear that he expects to have a share of the sandwiches even if the other party concerned isn't very anxious to sample the hay!

Pit ponies are stabled underground – often very near the shaft – but in mines where the workings extend a long way, the stables are often one mile or sometimes two from the shafts. This enables the ponies to live near their work. The stables are lit by electricity and have concrete floors, brick walls and the roof is supported by steel girders. The stables are whitewashed regularly and ponies stand tied in stalls separated by a brick partition from their stable companions.

Each groom, or horsekeeper must not have more than fifteen ponies under his charge. He is employed entirely in the stables and is responsible for their grooming, feeding, watering and welfare generally. One farrier serves about forty or fifty ponies: the shoeing is done cold and a large stock of ready-made shoes in varying sizes is kept.

If a pony falls sick he is put into a special loose-box but it is obviously better policy not to have sick ponies and prevention is better than cure. On an average, each pony's working conditions and stables are inspected at least four times a year by the Government Inspector, and a qualified veterinary surgeon looks the ponies over at least once, usually twice or even more often during the year. Working conditions are under constant supervision by the colliery staff and daily reports, made by the horsekeeper, ensure that the full story about each pony is kept up to date.

Food depends on size. A typical ration for a hard-working pony of between ten and eleven hands would be $6\frac{1}{2}$ lb chopped hay (from which dust has been extracted by machinery), 4 lb crushed oats, $\frac{1}{2}$ lb bran, 1 lb horse feed cake, and $\frac{1}{4}$ lb beans or molasses.

Although ponies sometimes come to the surface at holiday time, or in the event of sickness, it has been found better to keep them in the stable underground at a temperature and under conditions to which they are accustomed. You may think it is hot and stuffy underground but – generally speaking – the temperature in a stable is the same as that of a pleasantly warm summer's day. The average working life of a pit pony is nine years underground, although some ponies do live and work to a greater age.

In the early part of the century 70,000 ponies and horses were employed in the mines in Britain. It was just over a hundred years ago that horses first began to be used underground in mines and in those days they experienced some rough treatment. Although it may seem sad that any animal should be compelled to work away from daylight and in confined quarters, perhaps this account of how the pit pony lives will reassure you that he is usually well cared for and contented.

A GOOD TRAINER

by Josephine Pullein-Thompson

To be a good trainer it is necessary to possess a moderate amount of courage, a great deal of patience, and to love and understand horses.

The courage is necessary because, as the saying tells us, 'fear runs down the reins' and young horses recognize it at once and misbehave according to the dictates of their natures. Also, although the good trainer will try to achieve mastery tactfully and make obedience a habit rather than a due extracted by force, there comes a time in many a young horse's education when he rebels. Usually he refuses to do something he has done hundreds of times before. He will not leave the stable or he refuses to go down a track on a familiar ride. If, at this moment, the trainer feels the least qualm of fear the horse will know and the tentative attempt at disobedience may develop into a battle. When training a horse everything should be done to avoid battles, but if the trainer gets involved in one he must sit it out and win, otherwise he will take home a spoiled horse.

Patience is essential, because horses learn nothing if they are upset or over-excited and nothing upsets them like an impatient or bad-tempered rider. Apart from patience with the individual pupil, the whole programme of horse education calls for calm perseverance. Not only must each lesson be learned before the next is attempted, but time has to be allowed for the horse's muscles to develop; an untrained horse cannot be forced to carry out advanced movements any more than an ordinary person can perform the movements of a ballet.

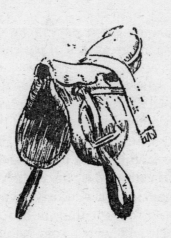

A FEW POISONS

Watch out that these poisons are kept away from your pony

Yew: The whole tree (leaves, bark, twigs) is dangerous. The pony often dies within five minutes of eating part of it.

Ragwort: Most experts consider this plant more poisonous when dead or wilting, so never pull up or cut it and then leave it lying about the field. It can also be deadly when eaten in hay.

Privet: Can be deadly when eaten in any quantity.

Bracken: Particularly if eaten in its green state, causes vitamin B1 deficiency. This can be cured if noticed in the early stages.

Acorns: Contain a lot of Tannic acid. Eating them is not usually fatal but causes severe colic.

Paint: Causes lead poisoning which is often fatal; so NEVER leave paint tins about the field.

If you think your pony has been poisoned send for a vet *at once*.

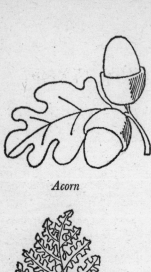

Acorn

Bracken

Privet

Yew

Ragwort

AN ABC OF EQUESTRIAN TERMS

by Alan Deacon
(including some rather unusual ones! Ed)

Equestrian terms are sometimes misleading, sometimes amusing, but rarely self-explanatory. This ABC contains most of those in regular use and some that are less often heard. I have not included all the many terms connected with specialist branches of horsemanship such as racing, and the expressions used by the driving fraternity, nor those confined to local regions.

AGED: A horse or pony over nine years old is said to be aged.

AIDS: The means at the disposal of the rider to convey his wishes to the horse.

ANGLO-ARAB: The produce of a pure-bred Arab mated with a thoroughbred. Such animals may be registered in the Anglo-Arab Stud Book. Not to be confused with Part-Bred Arab, which may be the produce of any horse or pony crossed with an Arab, or the offspring of these animals.

ASKING THE QUESTION: Putting the horse to a real test, e.g. a big jump or a tight finish in a race.

BABBLER: A hound who gives tongue when not on the scent of a fox.

BACKING: Mounting a horse for the first time. This term also refers to betting on races. Both things are a bit of a gamble!

BANG-TAIL: An undocked horse with a full tail that has been trimmed level with the hocks.

BARS: In this book this refers to the part of the horse's mouth between the incisor teeth and the molars, not somewhere to drink.

BILLETS: The Ds on a head collar, stud fasteners on reins and bridles. The droppings of a fox.

BINDER: A newly cut and laid fence with sticks laced along the top, also called 'stake and bound'.

BISHOPING: An old term for a practice adopted by unscrupulous people to make the teeth of an old horse appear to be those of a five- or six-year-old. The teeth of the lower jaw are rasped down, hollowed and burned black, then filled with 'dentist's cement'. Supposedly first done by a man called Bishop – or perhaps by a Bishop.

BLOOD HORSE: A thoroughbred, i.e. a horse with both sire and dam registered in the General Stud Book. A half-bred or threequarter-bred is a horse by a thoroughbred sire from a part-bred mare or from a mare of unknown breeding.

BLOODING: The ceremony at which a child is dabbed on the cheeks with blood from the fox's brush and then presented with the brush, after riding well throughout a hunt.

BOLT: A horse running away in absolute panic is bolting. One that eats quickly, without chewing its food properly, is said to bolt its food. To bolt a fox is to make it leave its earth by putting terriers down.

BONE: A horse with fine dense bone about eight or eight-and-a-half inches in diameter below the knee is said to have good bone. Hard, frosty ground has 'bone' in it.

BREAK: The early training of a horse is called breaking. A fox leaving covert 'breaks covert'. When hounds kill a fox they 'break it up'.

BREAKING OUT: A cold sweat sometimes breaks out on a horse in the stable after work, and after it has been dried off. This is the result of excitement, nervousness or overwork. Not to be confused with the ordinary sweating of a horse brought home hot.

Except on very cold days or when it is raining, a horse should be walked for the last quarter of an hour, otherwise he may break out as soon as he is put into the stable. If it is raining it will help you to dry the horse off if you trot right into the yard.

BREAST-PLATE AND BREAST-GIRTH: A breast-plate consists of a neck strap, which buckles on to Ds on the front of the saddle, and a further strap passing from a ring, down between the horse's forelegs and round the girth. A breast-girth is usually made of webbing, passes round the front of the horse, and is fastened either to the girth straps or a roller. It may have a strap passing over the front of the withers to prevent it hanging too low. The purpose of both items is to prevent the saddle or roller slipping back.

BROKEN WIND: A lung complaint affecting the horse's wind very badly. Incurable.

BRUSH: The tail of a fox. A 'brush' fence or 'fly' fence is made of bundles of birch or gorse packed into a wooden framework. 'Fly fence' can also refer to any jumpable hedge.

BRUSHING: A horse that knocks his leg with the opposite foot is brushing.

BULL: A horse that grunts when tested for soundness of wind, by a person threatening to strike its ribs, is sometimes called a bull.

BULLFINCH: A tall rough hedge. It may be possible to jump or scramble through the top of it.

BULL GROOM: A derogatory term used to describe a groom who is untidy in his work or so bad that other grooms regard him as only fit to look after cattle.

BURRO: Spanish word meaning donkey. Burra – she-ass. Often used as insults.

BUTCHER OR BUTCHER BOY: A rider with poor hands; one who jogs the horses mouth, knocks the animal about, who over-rides it; lacking in horse sense and the art of equitation.

BUTCHER BOY TROT: Trotting too fast.

CARTY: A common-bred horse, lacking quality.

CATCH HOLD: A horse that pulls is said to catch hold. Can also mean to collect and shake up a horse.

CAST: A horse 'thrown' for an operation. A horse that has 'got down' in the stable and cannot get up again without assistance. The effort made by hounds to pick up a scent. The huntsman 'casts' hounds when helping them to do this.

CAST SHOE: A shoe that has come off.

CHARLES JAMES: Name sometimes given to the fox; after King Charles II, regarded by some as cunning as a fox.

CHURN BARREL: Well-ribbed-up, roomy animal. Usually applied to brood mares with well-sprung ribs.

CLASS HORSE: A high-quality animal. T.B. of classic race ability.

CLASSIC RACES: The 2,000 Gns, 1,000 Gns, Derby, Oaks, and St Leger.

CLEAN BRED: Thoroughbred, pure Arab, or any horse or pony of pure breed.

CLEAN LIMBS: Limbs with no blemishes or scars, free from coarse hair.

CLINCH: Horse-shoe nail. A risen clinch – the end of the nail protruding outwards and upwards from the wall of the foot and should be knocked down.

CLICK OR CLICKING: Sound mad by the rider's tongue to urge horse on.

CLOTHING: Rugs, boots, bandages, etc.

COB: An animal of stocky build, fourteen to fifteen hands one inch. Cobby; stock of stocky build but above or below these measurements.

COLD BACK: A horse that humps its back when the saddle is put on or when mounted is cold backed.

COLT: A young entire horse or pony (i.e. not gelded) up to four years old. This term is often incorrectly applied to young geldings.

COMMON: A horse or pony lacking in quality.

CONFIDENTIAL: Horse or pony that is dead quiet at all times, with no tricks. One suitable for a novice or elderly person.

COPER: Dealer in horses and ponies.

COUPLE: Hounds are counted in couples. Two hounds equals one couple.

COUPLES: Collars joined with metal links to couple hounds together.

COVERT: A wood, patch of gorse or any place that holds a fox above ground.

CRAB: To pass unfavourable criticism.

CRUPPER: A strap passing from the saddle along the pony's back and under his dock to prevent the saddle slipping forward. More commonly used with driving harness or breaking tackle, and on very fat ponies.

CUTTING: Castrating (the gelding of a male horse or pony).

DAISY CUTTER: A horse with low, sweeping action.

DEFENCES: The means adopted by the horse in opposition to the rider.

DISHING: Throwing the feet outwards; opposite of brushing.

DO: To 'do' a horse is to groom him; may also refer to the complete daily care of the horse. Stable lads are said to 'do their two', although nowadays it is more often three than two that a lad does. A horse is said to 'do' or be a good 'doer' when he makes good use of the food he gets, thrives and puts on condition. A bad doer is the reverse of the above, in spite of good forage and care.

DONE: A horse whose grooming is complete. An exhausted horse. When a person has had the worst of a bad deal.

DRESSAGE: Means training.

DROPPING THE HANDS: Slackening the reins.

ENTER: To teach young hunters and hounds is to 'enter' them.

ENTIRE: A stallion; an un-gelded horse or pony; a full horse.

EXTEND: A long stride; a horse at its fastest pace.

FAULT: 'No fault', in writing is a warranty. If you buy a horse 'with all faults' you take the risk of latent faults and must calculate the price accordingly. 'You can't fault him' or 'he is hard to fault' are claims of perfection rather than actual warranties.

Hounds are 'at fault' when they cannot own the line.

FARRIER: A blacksmith who specializes in shoeing horses as against one who does other work such as repairing implements. A farrier will also have considerable veterinary knowledge.

FARTHINGALE: A decoration made from horse hair, often dyed with bright colours, which is suspended from the breast-plate. Used in ceremonial equipment, e.g. the drum horse of the Life Guards.

FAVOURING A LEG: An unsound horse throws as much weight as possible from the unsound leg on to the other legs. One that is not visibly unsound but has an 'if' will favour a leg.

FEATHER: Long hair below the knee and at the fetlocks.

FIGGING: The once common practice of inserting powdered ginger under the dock to make a horse carry its tail well and to give it temporary 'spirit' – gingering up, in fact. Jorrocks describing a nightmare said, 'I dreamt I was trying to sell Xerxes and forgot the ginger.'

FILLY: Female horse or pony up to four years old.

FLAPPER: Not a gay young thing, but a horse or pony raced at unauthorized (flapping) meetings, i.e. not under the rules of the Jockey Club (which includes point-to-points), or any recognized authority within, or outside, the British Isles, thereby barred from ever racing under rules, as also are jockeys, owners and trainers at flapping meetings.

FLAT CATCHER: A flashy, 'peacocky' horse, lacking substance, bone and stamina, likely to impress the inexperienced.

FOREHAND: The front, from withers to ears.

FORTY THIEVES: The gipsy and scrap-iron dealing fraternity who travel the round of horse fairs.

FOUR-IN-HAND: Four horses driven together in harness, e.g. a coach team.

FULL MOUTH: When a horse reaches six years of age he has a full mouth, i.e. all his adult teeth.

GENEROUS: A free-going horse which always does its best; bold and noble mean much the same thing.

GOOSE RUMPED: A slight arch at the end of the spine, near the dock.

GOING SHORT: Lame or going feelingly.

GREEN: Untrained or partly trained horse or pony.

GRUNTING TO THE STICK: Testing the horse's wind by threatening to strike his ribs. If he grunts he is 'touched' in the wind.

HACK: This term is confined to 'riding' horses other than racehorses, although in fact many show hacks have previously been racehorses. The show hack classes are divided into 'small hacks', exceeding 14.2 hands but not exceeding 15 hands, and 'large hacks', above 15 hands but not exceeding 15.3 hands. The good show hack is full of quality and presence, with extravagant action, and is perfectly trained. The impression given by hack and rider should be of great elegance combined with studied nonchalance.

HACK ON: To ride on to a meet or other venue.

HACKNEY: Breed of harness horses and ponies noted for high, vigorous action.

HANDS: Horses and ponies are measured in hands; four inches equal one hand.

When we speak of a rider having good hands, we are referring to the communication between rider and horse through the reins and in conjunction with the other aids. 'Mutton fisted' or 'ham fisted' means a clumsy rider.

HAND SALE: The shaking of hands to seal a deal. In horse dealing much business is done on mutual trust, the shaking of hands being sufficient to bind the parties to a deal often involving large sums of money.

HAUTE ECOLE: High school riding, exercises and movements that go beyond ordinary practical purposes.

HIRELING: A hack, hunter or pony hired out for profit; a riding-school horse.

HISSING: Grooms hiss when they are doing a horse to keep the dust out of their mouths, and sometimes to kid the guv'nor that they are busy.

HOBDAYED: A horse that has had an operation to the larynx to help its breathing has been Hobdayed. The operation was introduced by Professor Hobday.

HOLD HARD: This command means stop.

HONEST: A dependable horse.

HOSTLER OR OSTLER: Man in charge of inn stables, or any groom employed in such a stable.

IF: A suspicion or risk of unsoundness.

IN SEASON OR IN USE: A mare ready to receive a stallion.

JACK SPAVIN: Bone spavin.

JADE: A poor, uncourageous animal; a natural slug.

JAGGER: In this case not one of the Rolling Stones but a pack horse.

JAGGIN: A small load for a pack horse.

JOB HORSE: Vanners, coster's ponies, carriage horses, hired or 'jobbed' from a 'job master'.

JOB MASTERS: In the days before the coming of the motor-car, some job masters would have two hundred or more horses in regular work. Matched pairs for carriages and trade vans were in great demand and many business houses found it more economical and less trouble to hire their delivery horses from job masters. In the days of mail coaches the horses were supplied by 'horse contractors', which sounds very like a civil servant's name for a job master.

William Chapman, who began life as a coachman, was in his day the largest coach proprietor in London and in the world. With over 1,200 horses, he horsed fourteen of the twenty-seven coaches that left London every night.

Carter of Aberdeen had large stables with over 200 horses, but as far as I know he had little to do with coaches. Mr Palmer of Norwich was a famous job master, and his son Captain T. Palmer is a well-known horseman who used to buy large numbers of horses for the railway companies. The famous and still well-known firm of W. J. Smith Ltd had stables in London, Windsor and the West country, Miss Sybil Smith still carrying on her riding school at Maidenhead. There were of course literally hundreds of smaller job masters in London and throughout the country.

The job master had to maintain large numbers of horses and carriages of all descriptions, matched pairs and teams, large stocks of harness and a large staff, for he would sometimes be asked to provide drivers, footmen and grooms as well as the horses. As well as the regular jobbing of harness horses, job masters supplied large numbers of horses for the annual yeomanry camps, and sometimes horses would be jobbed to a master of hounds for the season. When the railways were being built hundreds of heavy horses and vanners were jobbed out to contractors.

JOBBING THE MOUTH: Jerking the horse's mouth with the bit.

JOCKEY CLUB: The controlling body of racing in Great Britain. An odd name since no professional jockey has ever been a member and many of the members have never ridden in races as amateurs.

JOG: A pace between walk and trot.

JOG TROT OR HOUND JOG: A slow trot, about six mph.

JUMPER'S BUMP: A prominent bump to the croup.

JORROCKS: The lovable character created by the sporting writer Surtees.

LAD: A stable lad might be any age. There is a delightful character study by the late Sir Alfred Munnings of 'Diadem's "lad" – aged 60'.

LIST: The black stripe that often runs down the back of a dun coloured horse, also known as a dorsal stripe.

LISK: The groin, particularly the place where the hair meets and runs in different directions.

LIVERPOOL HORSE: One capable of jumping the Grand National course at Aintree.

LIVERY: A horse for which feeding and stabling is paid for in a stable other than its owner's.

LONG IN THE TOOTH: An old horse, past mark of mouth when the black mark in the teeth which shows clearly up to seven years of age has vanished.

LOT OF HORSE IN A LITTLE ROOM: An animal standing close to the ground, well put together and bigger than it looks, measuring well and of good bone.

LUCK MONEY: It is traditional in horse dealing for the seller to give something back to the buyer or to throw something in for luck.

MADE: Broken-in and well schooled; experienced with hounds or in the ring or on the polo ground; well mannered and handy.

MAIDEN: A mare that has not been served by a stallion. Also can denote a racehorse that has not won a race.

MAKES A NOISE: Touched or unsound in wind.

MARE: Female horse or pony over four years old.

MARTINGALE: Strap or straps attached to nose band or reins and at other end to girth, to prevent the horse from carrying his head too high.

MASK: The head of a fox.

MEAT FOR MANNERS: Keep in return for use of the horse.

MEWS: Stable area in a town, often with grooms' flats above.

MILK TEETH: Foals are born with two incisors; these and the teeth which appear during the next eight months are milk teeth. The second pair come at about eight weeks and the third pair at about eight months. Later they are replaced by adult teeth.

MOUTHING: Teaching the young horse to accept the bit and to obey the signals given via bit and reins.

NAGGING: Schooling; making a horse handy and obedient.

NAGSMAN: A person who schools horses and rides them for exhibition to show them to their best advantage. In the old days all the big dealers employed first-class nagsmen. Famous among them was Robert Taylor. He won many prizes for Major Faudell Phillips including the Moscow Cup for hacks at Olympia twice. Later he became stud-groom and nagsman for Major Stewart Richardson at Dauntsey. Again he produced many show winners and good hunters and won the Moscow Cup three more times.

Equally famous and still in the front rank is Jack Gittins. He rode for the large establishment of Bert Drage between the wars. For many years now he has run his own establishment from which he produces a steady stream of top-class show winners and hunters. He has won many championships at Dublin riding Mr Nat Galway-Greer's horses. To see him schooling a young horse or riding across Leicestershire with consummate artistry is a sight to remember.

One cannot leave off the list such great showmen as

Sam Marsh and the late George Brine. Fortunately there are still some good nagsmen but there is a shortage of good professionals.

NAPPY: A cunningly rebellious horse.

NEAR SIDE: Left side.

NOBBLING: Doping or injuring a horse to prevent it winning.

OFF SIDE: Right side.

ON THE LEG: A tall horse; the inference being that the horse is too leggy and shows a lot of daylight under him.

OXER: A hedge with a guard rail in front of it; usually the rail is put up to prevent cattle poaching the sides of a ditch. A hedge with rails on both sides is a double oxer.

PARROT MOUTH: Upper teeth projecting over lower teeth.

PASSAGE: Highly cadenced, elevated trot with great collection, not to be confused with half-pass or full-pass.

PASS (half and full): The sideways and forward movement of a horse on two tracks. The feet must cross in front of each other and the neck should flex slightly in the direction to which the horse is moving. Should be carried out with good rhythm and plenty of impulsion. In the half-pass the horse moves forwards and sideways across the school at an angle of forty-five degrees and in the full-pass almost directly sideways.

PEACOCKY: A flashy horse; inclined to be cheeky.

PIAFFE: Similar to the passage, but marking time on the spot; there should be a moment of suspension as each diagonal is raised, and great flexion of the hocks as well as the knees is required.

PICK UP: To collect a horse and to ask him for an effort.

PIPE OPENER: A sharp gallop or canter to clear a horse's wind.

PLATER: A horse who runs in 'selling plates', races in which the winner is put up for auction immediately after the race.

PLATES: Light-weight shoes without toe clips, for racing and showing.

POINT-TO-POINT: A race for horses that have been regularly and fairly hunted, to be ridden by amateurs, and trained by amateurs, the only horses to be trained by a licensed trainer to be the property of that trainer or his wife. Three miles or more with fences of not less than four feet six inches. Originally run over natural country.

POSTING: The rising trot.

PROPPING: A horse that goes feelingly in front or one that slows up in the approach to a fence, perhaps trying to refuse.

PROPPY: Straight in front, i.e. shoulders and fore-limbs.

PUPPY WALK: Hound puppies, when weaned, are put out 'to walk'; the homes they are sent to are puppy walks and they remain at these walks until they are old enough to return to kennels and be entered with the pack.

PUT DOWN: To have an animal humanely destroyed.

PUT TO: To put a horse in harness to pull any type of

vehicle. A mare is 'put to' a stallion for service.

RASPER: A big fence.

RATE: To reprove hounds or horse.

RIG: An imperfectly castrated horse; although not capable of propagation rigs are a nuisance with mares.

ROACH BACK: Back with an upward curve; unsightly, and uncomfortable for the rider.

ROARER: A horse badly touched in its wind; not to be confused with 'high blowers', horses that flap the false nostril when cantering.

ROGUES BADGE: Blinkers worn by a racehorse.

ROUGHED OFF: Turned out to grass – not working.

SCREW: An inferior or unsound horse.

SECOND HORSE: Some lucky people hunt two horses a day, the second horse being brought on slowly by a second horseman. He should not take the second horse faster than a trot or hand canter, but must contrive to meet his master at the appointed time to change horses. A good second horseman needs an eye for a country, quick wits and a knowledge of hunting. Many famous huntsmen started their careers as second horsemen, graduating from that position to whipper-in and thence to the huntsman's post.

SET FAIR: A stable properly bedded down is set fair.

SOUND: A horse that is sound in wind, limb and eye. Jorrocks, when asked for a warranty, replied that he would not warrant the animal was a horse, let alone sound. In law 'sound' means free from hereditary disease and in possession of natural constitutional health.

SPARE LEG: A horse that recovers cleverly from a

jumping mistake is said to find a spare leg.

SPEEDY CUTTING: Striking the inside of the cannon high up with the opposite foot, usually when cantering or galloping, as against brushing where the leg is struck lower down.

SPIV: A groom unattached to a stable, who does spare or extra horses at a race meeting for trainers short of lads, also sees to boxing, etc of horses bought at sales.

STALE: Urination of a horse. A horse which is over trained is referred to as stale.

STAR GAZER: A horse who always carries his head too high.

STEEPLECHASE: A race over fences of four feet six inches or more in height, to include open ditches and a water jump, the distance of the race to be not less than two miles.

The early 'chases were run over natural hunting country.

The greatest steeplechase in the world is the Grand National, run at Aintree, Liverpool. The course is just over four and a half miles and there are thirty odd fences which are more formidable than most, many of them having considerable drops on the landing side. The Grand National is a handicap race, and considering the distance and the size of the fences, is run at a very fast pace.

The Cheltenham Gold Cup, run at level weights, is regarded as the 'classic of steeplechasing'.

The obstacles in hurdle races are made from sheep hurdles packed with gorse or birch bundles. The usual height is three feet nine inches.

STERN: The tail of a hound.

STICKY: An uncertain jumper; one that jumps from a standstill (cat jumping).

STINT: A right to pasture horses on common land. A mare that has been served by a stallion has been stinted.

STOCK: A hunting tie; usually white.

STRING: A number of horses belonging to one person or under the care of one person.

STRINGHALT: The snatching up of one hock abnormally high, a nervous complaint.

STUD: Breeding establishment or, a group of horses owned by one person.

SWAY BACK: Dipped back.

SWISHING TAIL: A sign of reluctance and/or resentment.

TACK: Stable requisites, saddles, bridles, etc.

TAKES HOLD: A horse that pulls or goes strongly into its bridle.

TAG: The white tip of a fox's brush.

TANDEM: Two horses driven together, one in front of the other, the wheeler in the shafts, the leader in traces.

T.B.: A thoroughbred horse, the sire and dam registered in the General Stud Book.

TRIPLE CROWN: A horse that wins the Guineas, Derby and St Leger wins the 'Triple Crown'.

THROW OFF: To send hounds into covert to draw for a fox. The other meaning is well known to us all!

THROW UP: Hounds throw up (their heads) when they have lost a fox and can do no more.

TUBED: A horse with a tracheotomy tube in its throat to aid its breathing.

TURNED OUT: A horse at grass. Well turned out means well groomed and presented. A 'turn out' means a horse-drawn vehicle plus horse and harness.

UNSEEN: A horse bought without being seen first by the purchaser is bought unseen. This is taking a bigger risk than warranting one for sale!

VANNER: A horse that pulls a light commercial vehicle.

VIXEN: Female fox.

VOLUNTARY: When we fall off we 'cut a voluntary'. I cannot think why as I have never volunteered to fall off.

WARRANTY: A form of guarantee.

WAXY: A saddler.

WEED: Horse possessed of little bone or substance.

WIND GALL: Puffy swelling on limb, caused by a blow.

WHISTLER: In this case not the artist, but a horse touched in its wind that makes a whistling noise when cantering and galloping; not as bad as a roarer.

WOLF TOOTH: When a second tooth does not grow immediately under a temporary tooth, but at its side, the tooth is pushed out of place and cuts the gum. The offending tooth is called a wolf tooth.

CROSSWORD 3

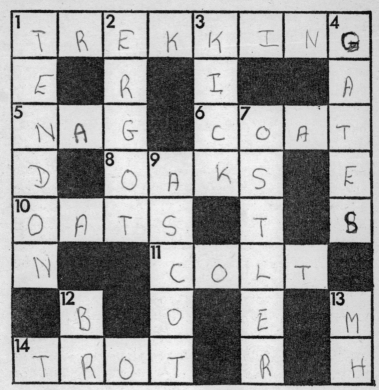

¹T	R	²E	K	³K	I	N	⁴G
E		R		I			A
⁵N	A	G		⁶C	⁷O	A	T
D		⁸O	⁹A	K	S		E
¹⁰O	A	T	S		T		S
N			¹¹C	O	L	T	
	¹²B		O		E		¹³M
¹⁴T	R	O	T		R		H

ACROSS

1. Cross-Country holiday riding (8)
5. Term for an old horse (3)
6. Your horse may have a staring — (4)
8. A race run at Epsom (4)
10. A good concentrated food (4)
11. A male under four years of age (4)
14. A pace (4)

DOWN

1. Part of the horse's leg (6)
2. A horny growth on fetlock joint (5)
3. Some horses may bite or — (4)
4. Can be jumped (5)
7. One who looked after horses stabled at an inn (6)
9. A race course (5)
12. Abbreviation for Brown (2)
13. Initials for Master of Harriers (2)

Answers on page 142.

WORKING WITH HORSES

by Christine Pullein-Thompson

Should you make a career of working with horses? The answer is don't, unless you cannot bear to do anything else. You need to be dedicated, courageous and to have strength and stamina. The hours may be long and week-ends off will be rare. You will be working in all weathers; you will often get up early and retire to bed late. Working with horses is a way of life. Make sure you like the life before you embark on it.

There are many different types of jobs in the riding world – groom, stable lad, riding instructor, stable man-ager, professional rider, trainer, jockey. You can work at a riding school, with show horses or jumpers, at a livery or racing stable, with polo ponies, at a trekking centre or a stud farm.

For the best jobs you need qualifications. A Pony Club A or B certificate is a good beginning. Or you can start as a working pupil at a riding school where you should receive instruction in exchange for work, and perhaps pocket money. But remember, if you do this, to choose a good school approved by The British Horse Society, with a qualified staff who will help you to become qualified yourself.

The recognized qualifications in Britain are the

certificates awarded by The British Horse Society. There are three levels awarded for instructors: the Assistant Instructor's (BHSAI), the Instructor's (BHSI) and the Fellowship (FBHS). And there are two levels for stable management: the BHS Horsemaster certificate and the BHS Stable Management certificate. The Pony Club also gives a special certificate for those wishing to work with horses. This, like the A and B certificate, is a great help when applying for your first job.

If you have no wish to become an expert at equitation, you may prefer to work at a trekking centre. Here you can be leader or groom. High qualifications may not be necessary, though some are certainly desirable. You will, as a leader, get plenty of riding amidst beautiful scenery. But do choose an approved centre, not the sort where ponies are over-worked and under-fed.

Working with show horses will mean a lot of travelling and perhaps sleeping in a horse-box or trailer. Some owners employ 'professional riders' to show their horses and occasionally to stay on through the winter preparing their young horses for the coming season. You will need showing experience for this sort of job.

Looking after polo ponies is usually a seasonal job and an excellent way of gaining experience. The ponies are generally kept at centres and this can be a pleasant summer occupation with a good deal of 'exercise riding'.

There is less riding with show jumpers, but a good chance of touring the shows and seeing the stars at close quarters.

Working on a stud farm may entail no riding, so

choose this only if you want to care for horses more than to teach or ride.

If you are the right sex and lightweight, you can try training as a jockey. You must weigh six stone or less at the age of fifteen and must never be much more than seven or eight stone when fully qualified. You begin by being an apprentice in direct agreement with a trainer; usually there is a trial period of about one or two months before indentures are signed. The normal period of apprenticeship is for five years and the indentures can only be broken by mutual consent. Unless you can already ride, you don't usually receive wages during apprenticeship, only pocket money, board and lodging, and personal clothing. However, the pocket money increases each year and if any horse in your charge wins a race you will be given something extra.

These are just a few of the jobs available. Instructors and stable managers are quite well paid. Grooms' wages tend to be low and based on an agricultural wage. There are plenty of fringe jobs such as secretary, mother's help, or general help at a residential centre where some riding may be available.

Jobs are advertised in riding papers and magazines, principally *Horse and Hound*. They can also be found through a few specialist agencies. For those who wish to travel, there are jobs in the United States and other parts of the world.

Finally, if you are determined to work with horses, discuss the prospects with your youth employment officer or your careers master. You may be able to apply for a grant from your Education Officer. This is entirely at the discretion of your local authority, but if you wish to train to be a riding instructor there is a real possibility of financial help. You can also apply to an educational charity for help. For the addresses of these consult the Annual Charities Register at your local library. For further information, write to The British Horse Society, National Equestrian Centre, Kenilworth, Warwickshire, CV8 2LP. They publish an excellent leaflet, entitled *A Career with Horses*, price 15p.

A PIG IN A POKE?

There was a young lady called Joan,
Who longed for a beautiful roan
She went to a sale,
And bought a fine male,
But soon after he died with a groan.

(Moral: Don't buy an unknown horse at a sale unless you
are an expert!)

QUIZ 3   FILL IN THE MISSING WORDS

1. A CRUPPER stops a saddle slipping forward. ✓
2. A jointed snaffle has a nut CRACKER action on a pony's mouth. ✓
3. When a pony has all his incisor teeth he is said to have a FULL mouth. ✓
4. A pony less than a year old is called a FOAL ✓
5. The Connemara is the native pony of IRELAND ✓
6. A pinkish or bluish, white eye is called a WALL EYE ✓
7. The lines and shape of your pony are called 'his CONFORMATION.' ✓
8. When you ride without a saddle it is called riding BARE BACK ✓
9. When a pony rushes past or round a jump after he has been told to jump, it is called RUNNING OUT
10. An Exmoor mare should not exceed 12·3 in height.
11. When you are a winner you are given a rosette. ✓
12. A pony of one year old is called a yearling ✓
13. A laid out collection of jumps is called a course ✗
14. In working hunter classes the horses entered are expected to jump. ✓
15. Wheat straw is an excellent form of BEDDING ✓
16. A race across country over jumps for horses regularly hunted is called a POINT TO POINT ✓

17. The club founded in 1929 to encourage and help young riders is called the PONY CLUB ✓

18. Rising at the trot can also be called POSTING ✓

19. Riders following hounds are called the FIELD

20. A person who buys and sells horses is called a horse DEALER

21. A hunting whip has a LASH on the end of its thong. ✗

22. A huntsman always carries a horn ✓

Answers on page 137.

From THE HOOVES OF HORSES

by Will H. Ogilvie

On the wings of the morning they gather and fly,
In the hush of the night time I hear them go by,
The horses of memory thundering through
With flashing white fetlocks all wet with the dew.

When you lay me to slumber no spot can you choose
But will ring to the rhythm of galloping shoes,
And under the daisies no grave be so deep
But the sound of the horses shall sound in my sleep.

And the last word from Norman Thelwell

In short – treat your pony as you like to be treated yourself

ANSWERS TO QUIZ 1
Which One Is Right?

1. (c)	7. (a)	13. (a)
2. (b)	8. (b)	14. (c)
3. (a)	9. (c)	15. (a)
4. (a)	10. (a)	16. (c)
5. (c)	11. (c)	17. (b)
6. (c)	12. (b)	

Three marks for each correct answer.
More than 60 marks – excellent
Less than 30 – you'd better start working!

ANSWERS TO QUIZ 2
You Name It

1. Shetland	13. A measuring stick
2. Curry comb	14. The forehand
3. Chestnut	15. Peat Moss
4. Cannon bone	16. Grass
5. Chaff	17. A stayer
6. Mare	18. A hoof pick
7. A stock	19. A pony
8. Hollow-backed	20. A girth gall
9. The wall	21. The meet
10. Cow hocks	22. Spur
11. Cold shoeing	23. The withers
12. A weed	24. Windgall

ANSWERS TO QUIZ 3
Fill in the Missing Words

1. Crupper
2. Cracker
3. Full
4. Foal
5. Ireland
6. Wall eye
7. Conformation
8. Bare-back
9. Running out
10. 12.2 hh.
11. Rosette
12. Yearling
13. Course
14. Jump
15. Bedding
16. Point-to-point
17. Pony Club
18. Posting
19. Field
20. Horse-dealer
21. Lash
22. Horn

WHAT JONATHAN DID WRONG

Jonathan rose too late from his bed on the morning of the ride. He fed himself before Seagull, leaving her no time to digest. He fed whole oats which are difficult for an elderly pony to chew and digest, and he fed her too many for a pony not normally fed oats.

Jonathan gave his pony little or no water. He rode her too hard during the day, never dismounting to give her back a rest. He should have led her some of the way home after such a hard day and walked the last mile so that she arrived cool and dry. On arrival he should have watered her before feeding. As it was, when she *was* eventually watered she drank too much too fast, no doubt washing the undigested whole oats straight into her intestines.

He failed to look her over for thorns, scratches, punctures or cuts which might easily have occurred on such a wild ride. All of these could turn septic or lead to tetanus if not treated in good time.

Nor did he visit Seagull later to see whether she was warm and comfortable after such a long and exhausting ride; if he had gone to see her, and, on finding her ill, sent for the vet, he might well have saved her life.

Jonathan fed Seagull too late on the following morning, leaving her ample time to eat frosted grass which can cause colic, so that when eventually he saw her, she had already twisted a gut and was doomed.

Jonathan's parents were also to blame for expecting anyone his age and experience to look after a pony unaided.

Lastly, though Seagull was elderly, Jonathan put himself first on every occasion.

TEST YOUR KNOWLEDGE

The objectives of grooming are:
    To keep your pony healthy.
    To improve his appearance.
    To keep him clean.
    To maintain condition.
    To stop disease.

The Dandy Brush is for removing mud and heavy dirt from your pony.

The Body Brush is for removing grease and dust from your pony's coat, mane and tail. It should not be used on a pony living out in the winter as he needs grease in his coat to keep him warm and dry.

The Curry Comb is used for cleaning the body brush.

The Hoof Pick is for cleaning out the hoofs.

The Water Brush is for damping mane, tail and hoofs.

The Sponge is for cleaning eyes, nostrils and dock.

The Wisp is for massage; helps to develop muscle and circulation.

The Stable Rubber is for polishing your pony after grooming.

Body brush

Curry comb

Water brush

Hoof pick

Stable rubber

Dandy brush

Sponge

Wisp

ANSWERS TO CROSSWORDS

Crossword 1

Across
1. Jumping   5. As   6. Colic   7. Halt   9. Ears
11. Stable   14. Shire
Down
1. Jockey   2. Molars   3. Itch   4. Gall   8. Tread
10. Star   12. Bl.   13. NH

Crossword 2

Across
1. Bridles   4. Eolúppus   5. Covert   8. At   9. Loins
11. Sit   12. Nose
Down
1. Breeches   2. Drive   3. Stud   6. Volt   7. Rein
8. Ass   10. No

Crossword 3

Across
1. Trekking   5. Nag   6. Coat   8. Oaks   10. Oats
11. Colt   14. Trot
Down
1. Tendon   2. Ergot   3. Kick   4. Gates   7. Ostler
9. Ascot   12. Br   13. MH